S0-BFB-762

Contents

Introduction v

01 / Beginning German 1
    Learn Your ABCs and How to Pronounce Them 1
    Sounds: Vowels, Consonants, and Combinations 2
    Numbers and Counting 9
    German in English, English in German 13
    Speak! Speak! Speak! 15

02 / Building Your Vocabulary 17
    Names and Titles 17
    Greetings and Goodbye's 19
    Countries and Nationalities 21
    Days and Dates 22
    Telling Time 26
    Family Members 29
    Basic Food and Eating Terms 31

03 / Grammar 35
    Intro to Grammar 35
    Understanding Gender 35
    Person, Place, or Thing? 36
    Articles Are Important 43
    Making Nouns Plural 45
    Pronouns 49
    Adjectives and Where They Stand 52
    Verbs: Infinitives, Auxiliaries, and Conjugations 54

Going Somewhere? Verbs of Motion 56
Present Tense. 59
Verbs That End in *–ieren* 60
Negation 62
Irregular Verbs. 63
Past Tense. 68
Future Tense. 76
Prefixes. 79
Direct Objects 82
Indirect Objects. 86

04 / Putting It All Together 93
Questions. 93
Commands 98
Express Yourself with Feeling Verbs 100
Idiomatic Expressions. 102
What's Yours? Possessives 103
Describing Things and People 108
Conjunctions: Ifs, Ands, and Buts 117

05 / Getting Around. 121
Securing a Room. 121
Around the House. 123
Kaffee und Kuchen 124
Modern Times and Technology in Germany. 125
Games and Sports 127
A Love for Animals 128
Paying with the Euro 129

Appendix A / German to English Dictionary 131
Appendix B / English to German Dictionary 159
Index 184

LEARN

German
in a Hurry

GRASP

THE BASICS OF

Deutsch

im Schnellgang!

Edward Swick

A**adams**media

Avon, Massachusetts

Published by
Adams Media, an F+W Publications Company
57 Littlefield Street, Avon, MA 02322 U.S.A.
www.adamsmedia.com

ISBN 10: 1-59869-549-5
ISBN 13: 978-1-59869-549-6

Printed in Canada.

J I H G F E D C B A

Library of Congress Cataloging-in-Publication Data
available from publisher.

This publication is designed to provide accurate and authoritative information with regard to the subject matter covered. It is sold with the understanding that the publisher is not engaged in rendering legal, accounting, or other professional advice. If legal advice or other expert assistance is required, the services of a competent professional person should be sought.
    —From a *Declaration of Principles* jointly adopted by a Committee of the American Bar Association and a Committee of Publishers and Associations

Many of the designations used by manufacturers and sellers to distinguish their product are claimed as trademarks. Where those designations appear in this book and Adams Media was aware of a trademark claim, the designations have been printed with initial capital letters.

Contains materials adopted and abridged from
The Everything® Learning German Book by Edward Swick,
Copyright © 2003 by F+W Publications, Inc.

*This book is available at quantity discounts for bulk purchases.
For information, please call 1-800-289-0963.*

Introduction

We live in a world where a lot of things go on at a very fast pace. Even language acquisition is often approached in a hurry. Well, if you're one of those people who need to learn some German quickly, this is the book for you. It doesn't matter if your goal for your new language is travel or business or just a personal interest in German. What's important is that you have the desire to learn, because that kind of attitude breeds success.

You'll find that the concepts contained in this book are presented in simple and clear language. Grammatical and linguistic terms are kept to a minimum and are fully explained when needed. You'll be briefed on the German alphabet and the sounds that are identical to English and the ones that are different. You'll be made aware of basic spelling rules, which in German are not complicated, because the language is—for the most part—written as it is pronounced.

Since German and English are brother and sister languages, you'll find many similarities between them, which is a distinct advantage when learning a new language. You probably don't even need the English translation to know what the following words mean.

- *finden* (find)
- *Auto* (auto)
- *braun* (brown)
- *mein* (mine)
- *singen* (sing)
- *Winter* (winter)

This doesn't mean that you'll breeze through everything though. It's just that the similarity between German and English make the learning process a little smoother and far less frustrating.

If you apply yourself and take the book seriously, you'll end up with the basics for spoken and written communication. The vocabulary you'll encounter are the essentials you need for travel, dining, shopping, and getting by in an urban setting in Germany. You'll have enough skill with the tenses to make sense when you talk about things that happened yesterday or things that will go on today and tomorrow. In general, you'll know enough German to form the basis that will allow you to communicate as an educated foreigner and that will be the first building block for further German study.

Viel Spaß! Have fun!

01 / Beginning German

Learn Your ABCs and How to Pronounce Them

The German alphabet (*das Alphabet*) is made up of the same letters that make up our English alphabet, with one exception. German has one letter that we do not have in English. It is called an "ess-tset" and is often mistaken for a capital "B." It looks like this (ß) and is pronounced like a double "s" (ESS). It takes the place of *ss* after long vowels or diphthongs. Note these examples: *heißen, groß, draußen*. The following table shows the pronunciation of the German alphabet. The new orthography has changed the rules for using ß.

▶ **Das Alphabet**

Letter	Pronunciation
A a	ah
Ä ä	ah Umlaut
B b	bay
C c	tsay
D d	day
E e	ay

F f	eff
G g	gay
H h	ha
I i	ee
J j	yawt
K k	kah
L l	ell
M m	em
N n	en
O o	oh
Ö ö	oh Umlaut
P p	pay
Q q	koo
R r	air
S s	ess
T t	tay
U u	oo
Ü ü	oo Umlaut
V v	fow
W w	vay
X x	ix
Y y	ypsilon
Z z	tset

Sounds: Vowels, Consonants, and Combinations

The descriptions that follow can serve as your guide as you practice forming German sounds. The English phonetics will be shown with the stressed syllable in capital letters, for example, *Vater* (FAH-tuh), and enclosed in parentheses.

Vowels

Hearing the sounds pronounced by a native will be helpful. Also you should be aware that when English phonetics are provided, there is no precise way to indicate the pronunciation of *Ö ö* and *Ü ü*. The phonetics will show their sounds as *er* (in bold letters) and *ue* (in bold letters) respectively.

An Umlaut is the two dots that sometimes appear over the letters "a," "o," and "u." They occur with no other letters. As you'll see in the next table, the Umlaut changes the pronunciation of the vowel sound slightly.

▶ **Pronouncing the Vowel Sounds**

Letter	Sound	Example	Pronunciation	Translation
A a	ah as in "father"	*Vater*	VAH-tuh	father
Ä ä	ay as in "say"	*spät*	SHPATE	late
E e	ay as in "say"	*Weg*	VAYK	path
I i	ee as in "tree"	*ich*	EECH	I
O o	o as in "go"	*Foto*	FOE-toe	photo
Ö ö	e as in "her"	*schön*	SHERN	beautiful
U u	oo in "moon"	*tut*	TOOT	does
Ü ü	Pucker lips to say "oo" but say "ee."	*Tür*	TUER	door
Y y	Pucker lips to say "oo" but say "ee."	*Gymnasium*	guem-NAH-zee-oom	high school

Long and Short Vowels

Just as in English, there is a slight difference between long and short vowels in German. The words "long" and "short" are an accurate description of the difference between the sounds in German. Long vowels are drawn out more when pronounced. They tend to precede a single consonant. Short vowels usually precede a double consonant and are pronounced more quickly.

▶ Long Vowel Sounds Before a Single Consonant

German Word	Pronunciation of Vowel	Pronunciation of Word	Translation
Vater	long ah	VAH-tuh	father
Käse	long ay	KAY-zeh	cheese
Keks	long ay	KAYKS	cracker
grob	long oh	GROP	rude
schön	long er	SHERN	beautiful
gut	long oo	GOOT	good
spülen	long oo Umlaut	SHPUE-len	to flush

▶ Short Vowel Sounds Before a Double Consonant

German Word	Pronunciation of Vowel	Pronunciation of Word	Translation
Halle	short uh	HUH-leh	hall
fällen	short eh	FELL-en	to chop down
Keller	short eh	KELL-uh	basement
Zoll	short aw	TSAWL	custom
können	short er	KER-nen	to be able to
Mummel	short oo	MOOM-ell	waterlily
müssen	short oo Umlaut	MUESS-en	to have to

You must look at the form of a word to determine whether the phonetic spelling "oo" is long or short: *Mutter* (MOO-tuh) (short "oo" because it precedes a double consonant) or *tun* (TOON) (long "oo" because it precedes a single consonant).

Pronouncing the Consonants

German consonants are pronounced fairly close to how they are pronounced in English. The next table will show you how to pronounce the consonants in German words.

▶ **Pronouncing the Consonants**

Letter	Pronunciation	Example	Pronunciation	Translation
B b	b as in "baby"	*Buch*	BOOCH	book
C c	ts as in "bits"	*Cent*	TSENT	cent
D d	d as in "did"	*Doktor*	DAWK-tuh	doctor
F f	f as in "fit"	*fein*	FINE	fine
G g	g as in "goggles"	*gut*	GOOT	good
H h	h as in "hat"	*Haus*	HOUSE	house
J j	y as in "yard"	*ja*	YAH	yes
K k	k as in "kick"	*Kind*	KINT	child
L l	l as in "little"	*bellen*	BELL-en	to bark
M m	m as in "mama"	*Mutter*	MOO-tuh	mother
N n	n as in "noon"	*nicht*	NIHCHT	not
P p	p as in "papa"	*Preis*	PRICE	prize
Q q	kv as in "back vent"	*Quelle*	KVELL-eh	source
R r	guttural similar to French "r"	*rot*	ROT	red
S s	s as in "sis" middle of a word	*Meister*	MYE-stuh	master
S s	z as in "zap" start of a word	*soll*	ZAWL	ought to
T t	t as in "toot"	*tun*	TOON	to do
V v	eff as in "fit"	*vier*	FEER	four
V v	v as in "very" usually foreign	*Vase*	VAH-zeh	vase

	words			
W w	v as in "Vivian"	*Walter*	VAHL-tuh	the name Walter
X x	x as in "wax"	*verflixt*	fare-FLIKST	tricky
Z z	ts as in "bits"	*Zoll*	TSAWL	custom

There are a few things you have to look out for with certain consonants, besides what's given in the table above. Sometimes the consonants change sound, depending on their placement in a word, as you can already see from the pronunciation for the letter "s." Here are a few more rules you'll need to know about pronunciation.

When the letter "b" appears at the end of a word or prefix, it is pronounced like a "p."

▶ **Sounding the Letter "B" at the End of a Word or Prefix**

German	Pronunciation	English
grob	GROP	rude
starb	SHTAHRP	died
ablehnen	AHP-lay-nen	to reject
absagen	AHP-zah-gen	to cancel

When the letter "d" appears at the end of a word, it is pronounced like a "t."

▶ **Sounding the Letter "D" at the End of a Word or Prefix**

German	Pronunciation	English
Deutschland	DOITCH-lunt	Germany
Freund	FROINT	friend
Kind	KINT	child
Gold	GAWLT	gold
Geld	GELT	money
Bild	BILLT	picture

When the letter "g" appears at the end of a word or prefix, it is pronounced like a "k."

▶ Sounding the Letter "G" at the End of a Word or Prefix

German	Pronunciation	English
Weg	VAYK	path
lag	LAHK	lay
trug	TROOK	wore
weglaufen	VEHK-low-fen	to run away

Letter Combinations

German pronunciation is also affected by groups of letters. Certain combinations of letters have their own sounds that you must be aware of. When two vowels in the same syllable form one speech sound, it is called a diphthong.

▶ Pronouncing Combined Letters and Diphthongs

Letters	Sound	Example	Pronunciation	English
AA	ah as in "father"	Saal	ZAHL	salon, hall
AU	ow as in "cow"	Frau	FROW	woman
EU	oi as in "toil"	Heu	HOI	hay
ÄU	oi as in "toil"	Fräulein	FROI-line	young woman
EI	i as in "high"	klein	KLINE	small
IE	ee as in "feet"	tief	TEEF	deep
EE	ay as in "say"	Tee	TAY	tea
ER	air as in "stair"	merken	MAIR-ken	to notice

Letters	Sound	Example	Pronunciation	English
ER	at the end of words only uh as in British "father"	Messer	MESS-uh	knife
OO	o as in "home"	Boot	BOT	boat
CH	guttural ch as in Scottish loch	Koch	KOCH	cook
CHS	x as in "wax"	sechs	ZEHKS	six
SCH	sh as in "shush"	Schuh	SHOO	shoe
TSCH	ch as in "church"	Deutschland	DOITCH-lunt	Germany
SP	shp as in "cash payment"	Sport	SHPORT	sport
ST	sht as in "wash tub"	stark	SHTAHRK	strong
TH	t as in Tom	Bibliothek	beeb-lee-oh-TAKE	library
PF	pf as in "top fin"	Pfennig	PFENN-ik	penny

Many words in German have an "h" directly following a vowel. That "h" is most often silent. For example, *gehen* (to go) is not GAY-hen. It is pronounced GAY-en.

It is also to be noted that the German *–ch* resembles the guttural Scottish *–ch*.

▶ **Pronouncing Words with an "H" Following a Vowel**

German	Pronunciation	English
fliehen	FLEE-en	to flee
glühen	GLUE-en	to make red hot
sehen	ZAY-en	to see
stehen	SHTAY-en	to stand

There is also no English equivalent for German *ch* (guttural like Scottish *ch*). It will be shown phonetically as *ch* (in bold letters) and should not be confused with the English version of that letter combination.

Numbers and Counting

Knowing how to use numbers in German is important. You may have already heard people counting in German, and now it's your turn to take a crack at German numbers. The first thing you'll want to learn is counting to ten.

▶ **Numbers 0–10**

Arabic Numeral	German Number	Pronunciation
0	*null*	NOOL
1	*eins*	AYNTZ
2	*zwei*	TSVY
3	*drei*	DRY
4	*vier*	FEAR
5	*fünf*	**FUE**NF
6	*sechs*	ZEX
7	*sieben*	ZEE-ben
8	*acht*	AH**CH**T
9	*neun*	NOIN
10	*zehn*	TSAYN

You use *eins* as "one" only when counting or when the number stands alone. Once it stands in front of a noun, the –*s* is dropped and it is treated just like *ein* and *eine,* the indefinite articles. Therefore, *ein Mann* can mean either "a man" or "one man."

Look at some sentences that use the numbers 1–10.

- *Hier wohnen zwei Amerikaner.* (Two Americans live here.)
- *Der alte Mann hat zehn Wagen.* (The old man has ten cars.)
- *Sechs Schüler fahren mit dem Bus zur Schule.* (Six pupils take the bus to school.)

The Next Ten

The next ten numbers are just as simple to use as the first ten. You'll see that 13–19 use a combination of *zehn* (10) and one of the numbers you just learned.

▶ **Numbers 11–20**

Arabic Numeral	German Number	Pronunciation
11	elf	ELF
12	zwölf	TSV**ER**LF
13	dreizehn	DRY-tsayn
14	vierzehn	FEAR-tsayn
15	fünfzehn	F**UE**NF-tsayn
16	sechzehn	ZEX-tsayn
17	siebzehn	ZEEP-tsayn
18	achtzehn	AH**CH**T-tsayn
19	neunzehn	NOIN-tsayn
20	zwanzig	TSVAHN-tsik

When asking the question "how much," you say *wie viel* (vee-FEEL).

- *Wie viel ist zwei plus zwei?* (How much is two plus two?)
- *Wie viel ist sechs und zwei?* (How much is six and two?)

■ *Wie viel ist neun weniger drei?* (How much is nine minus three?)

The Rest of the Numbers

The numbers from one to twenty are the basis for learning the rest of the numbers in German. To make that process easier, keep in mind a line from a children's rhyme: "Four-and-twenty blackbirds baked in a pie." As you learn the numbers above twenty, you'll see why this rhyme is fitting for putting together numbers in German. First let's look at the numbers for counting by tens to a hundred.

▶ Counting by Tens

Arabic Numeral	German Number	Pronunciation
10	*zehn*	TSAYN
20	*zwanzig*	TSVAHN-tsik
30	*dreißig*	DRY-sik
40	*vierzig*	FEAR-tsik
50	*fünfzig*	F**UE**NF-tsik
60	*sechzig*	ZEK-tsik
70	*siebzig*	ZEEP-tsik
80	*achtzig*	AH**CH**-tsik
90	*neunzig*	NOIN-tsik
100	*hundert*	HOON-duhrt

Just as happened in the teens, *sechzig* has dropped the letter *–s* from *sechs,* and in *siebzig* the syllable *–en* has been omitted from *sieben.*

The hundreds are even easier to form. Note that with the hundreds, the forms of *sechs* and *sieben* do NOT drop any letters.

▶ The Hundreds

Arabic Numeral	German Number
100	*hundert*
200	*zweihundert*
300	*dreihundert*
400	*vierhundert*
500	*fünfhundert*
600	*sechshundert*
700	*siebenhundert*
800	*achthundert*
900	*neunhundert*
1,000	*tausend*

The same pattern follows in the thousands: *zweitausend, zehntausend,* and so on.

Here's where the blackbirds come in: With twenty through ninety, the numbers one through nine are placed *before* the rest of the number and connected by *und:*

- *einundzwanzig* (21, literally "one-and-twenty")
- *zweiundzwanzig* (22)
- *vierunddreißig* (34)
- *fünfundfünfzig* (55)
- *sechsundsiebzig* (76)
- *siebenundneunzig* (97)

When using *eins,* don't forget to drop the –*s* in this formation of numbers: *einundvierzig, einundachtzig.*

The larger numbers in German are almost identical to English. (But be on guard: There's a notable exception to watch for.) And these larger numbers are capitalized. The other numbers are not.

▶ **Numbers for Billionaires**

English Number	German Number	Example
million	*eine Million* mee-lee-OHN	*zehn Millionen Dollar*
billion	*eine Milliarde* mee-lee-AHR-deh	*drei Milliarden EUR*
trillion	*eine Billion* bee-lee-OHN	*sechs Billionen Pesos*

Careful! If you're a billionaire, you have to be aware of how German and English differ when it comes to billions and trillions. Take another look at the table above and check out the meaning of *Milliarde* and *Billion*.

German in English, English in German

German and English share many words in common. These are called cognates and are found in most European languages. Here are just a few German words you will recognize immediately.

▶ **Words You'll Recognize**

German	Pronunciation
abstraktiv	ahb-strahk-TEEF
die Adresse	DEE ah-DRESS-eh
aktiv	ahk-TEEF
der Artist	DAIR ahr-TEEST
das Auto	DUSS OW-toh
das Baby	DUSS BAY-bee
der Boss	DAIR BAWSS
die Chance	DEE SHAWN-tseh
der Club	DAIR KLOOP
der Computer	DAIR kawm-PYOO-tuh
cool	KOOL

der Dealer	DAIR DEE-leh
der Diplomat	DAIR dee-ploh-MAHT
fair	FARE
der Film	DAIR FILM
das Hotel	DUSS hoh-TELL
der Job	DAIR JAWP
das Land	DUSS LUNT
der Manager	DAIR MEH-neh-juh
der Name	DAIR NAH-meh
national	nah-tsee-oh-NAHL
negativ	nay-guh-TEEF
offensiv	aw-fen-SEEF
der Optimist	DAIR ohp-tee-MEEST
der Pessimist	DAIR pess-ee-MEEST
die Physik	DEE **fueh**-ZEEK
der Pilot	DAIR pee-LOHT
plus	PLOOS
positiv	poh-zee-TEEF
das Problem	DUSS proh-BLAME
der Professor	DAIR pro-FESS-uh
relativ	ray-luh-TEEF
das Restaurant	DUSS ress-taw-RONG
das Shopping	DUSS SHAW-peeng
die Specials	DEE SPEH-shulls
das System	DUSS **zue**ss-TAME
der Terrorist	DAIR tare-ohr-REEST
die Tradition	DEE trah-dee-tsee-OWN

Cognates in Context

There are so many shortcuts to learning new German words. Following are a few sentences using some words that will probably look familiar to you. Don't worry about understanding the sentence structure yet—this will get you used to looking at written German. Can you pick out the meanings of any of the words used?

- *Andreas gewinnt einen Preis.* (Andreas wins a prize.)
- *Meine Familie ist sehr klein.* (My family is very little.)
- *Petra spielt Gitarre.* (Petra plays guitar.)
- *Wir lieben die Natur.* (We love nature.)
- *Morgen gehen wir in die Oper.* (Tomorrow we're going to the opera.)
- *Das ist perfekt!* (That's perfect!)
- *Das ist eine dumme Theorie!* (That's a dumb theory!)
- *Er braucht Salz und Pfeffer.* (He needs salt and pepper.)
- *Deine Schwester ist sehr attraktiv.* (Your sister is very attractive.)
- *Warum bist du so nervös?* (Why are you so nervous?)
- *Ich trinke keinen Kaffee.* (I don't drink coffee.)
- *Jazz ist sehr populär.* (Jazz is very popular.)

Speak! Speak! Speak!

No language—not German, not English, not Japanese —evolved from a written form. Writing came later. Speech came first. Language is first and foremost a spoken form. And to know German well, you have to be able to speak it. Translating words in your mind isn't good enough. You have to pronounce words and phrases and sentences out loud in order to learn German speech. Here's the basic rule, and it's quite simple: In order to learn to speak German, you have to practice speaking German.

It's like playing the piano. Let's say you want to be a pianist. So you get some sheet music and begin studying it. You look at all the notes and memorize what they're called: do, re, mi, fa, sol, la, ti, do. You study the phrasing and key signatures. But you don't touch a single key on the piano. After six months of study, when you finally lay your hands on the keyboard, you will still not be a pianist. Because it doesn't work that way.

And that's true with language acquisition as well. In order to learn to speak German, you have to practice speaking German. Follow that rule, and in time you will be speaking German with ease.

02 / Building Your Vocabulary

Names and Titles

Just like English speakers, Germans address one another with first names on an informal basis and with a title and last name on a formal basis. The list of first and last names that follows contains many names already familiar to you.

Andreas (ahn-DRAY-us)	*Bauer* (BOW-uh)
Brandt (BRAHNT)	*Brenner* (BRENN-uh)
Gerhardt (GAIR-hart)	*Gretchen* (GRATE-**ch**en)
Hans (HAHNS)	*Herbert* (HAIR-bayrt)
Müller (MUEL-luh)	*Schmidt* (SHMITT)

German has shortened first names or nicknames just as English does. In America, Robert can be called Bob, and John can be called Jack. Susie is just the shortened version of Susanne.

In Germany, the same thing happens. *Johann* is known to his friends as *Hans*. *Margarethe* is *Gretchen* or *Gretel*. *Eduard* becomes *Edu*. *Geli* comes from *Angelika*. And sometimes a double first name borrows a syllable from each name to form a nickname: *Lieselotte* becomes *Lilo*.

You should be aware of such shortened names or nicknames, but don't try using them until you have more experience with the language. Although the English name Richard is also the German name *Richard,* you cannot refer to *Richard* as *Dick.* The German word *dick* means "fat"!

When using a last name, you should use the appropriate title of the person to whom you are speaking.

▶ **Titles in German Names**

German	Pronunciation	English Equivalent
Herr	HAIR	mister
Frau	FROW	Ms.
Doktor	DAWK-tuh	(academic) doctor
Professor	proh-FESS-uh	professor

Germany went through something of a women's liberation movement about the same time the United States did. There were various outcomes of that movement, and one of them was a significant change in the language.

That change turned the word *Fräulein* into a taboo word. It's a diminutive form of *Frau* that actually means "little lady" or "little woman." It once was used as the title "Miss" to address a young or unmarried woman. Just as our word "Miss" has fallen out of grace, so, too, has the word *Fräulein* become a cultural no-no.

Nowadays, you should use *Frau* with all women—married, single, young, and old. As a foreigner, you'll be forgiven if you forget and say *Fräulein,* but it's only polite to strive to use the correct form.

Greetings and Goodbye's

To say "hello" to someone, you use the phrase *Guten Tag* (GOO-ten TUCK). For example, when saying hello to *Andreas,* you would say, *"Guten Tag, Andreas." Guten Tag* literally means "good day." You have probably heard this common German greeting before. But it's typically used to greet someone only during the afternoon. At other times of the day you have to say something else.

In the morning hours you should say *Guten Morgen* (MAWR-gen), which means "good morning." In the afternoon you say *Guten Tag.* In the evening use *Guten Abend* (AH-bent), which means "good evening." And late at night you say *Gute Nacht* (NAH**CH**T), or "good night," which, just like in English, is a way of saying "good-bye."

Did you know that Germans shake hands when they greet someone or say good-bye to someone? You may think that sounds just like what Americans do, and to some extent that's true. But Germans consider it almost a rule.

Now for the farewell. Most English speakers already know that Germans say good-bye with the phrase *auf Wiedersehen* (OWF VEE-duh-zane). But it really doesn't mean "good-bye." A closer translation is "till I see you again."

But there is another form of good-bye that is very commonly used, although mostly with good friends. It is very casual. It comes from a long time past when it was fashionable to use the French word when bidding farewell to friends: *adieu.* In the course of time, and with people from all over the German-speaking world pronouncing and mispronouncing the word, it somehow got an *s* attached to it. Then it lost its first syllable. And in time it became simply *Tschüs* (CHUESS).

You can't go wrong by saying *auf Wiedersehen,* but it's fun using *Tschüs* when the occasion allows for it: in casual circumstances or saying good-bye to friends.

When you say that someone is going home, use the following phrase:

■ *Andreas geht jetzt nach Hause.* (Andreas is going home now.)

Any name can be substituted for *Andreas.* And when someone is going home, it's an appropriate time to wish him or her *auf Wiedersehen* or *Tschüs.*

If you're speaking on the phone, you don't use *auf Wiedersehen* to say good-bye. That's only for when you see someone face-to-face. When saying good-bye on the phone, use *auf Wiederhören* (OWF VEE-duh-her-ren). It means something like "till I hear your voice again."

How Are You?

When asking how someone is doing, you first have to decide whether you're on a casual or formal basis with the person. Usually, if you're using someone's first name, you have a casual or informal relationship with that person. If you're using a title and last name, you have a formal relationship with that person.

Casual: "How are you?" *"Wie geht's, Andreas?"* (VEE GATES)
Formal: "How are you?" *"Wie geht es Ihnen, Herr Braun?"* (VEE GATE ESS EE-nen)

Countries and Nationalities

Learning the names of countries, nationalities, and languages is a quick way to add an abundance of new words to your vocabulary. The following table shows the names of several countries, the names for citizens (male and female, respectively) of those countries, and the language spoken there. Notice how similar many of the words are to English words.

▶ Countries, Nationalities, and Languages

Das Land *(country)*	Die Nationalität *(nationality)*	Die Sprache *(language)*
Belgien (Belgium)	*der Belgier, die Belgierin*	*Französisch* (French)
China	*der Chinese, die Chinesin*	*Chinesisch*
Deutschland	*der Deutsche, die Deutsche*	*Deutsch*
England	*der Engländer, die Engländerin*	*Englisch*
Frankreich (France)	*der Franzose, die Französin*	*Französisch*
Italien	*der Italiener, die Italienerin*	*Italienisch*
Japan	*der Japaner, die Japanerin*	*Japanisch*
Niederlande (The Netherlands)	*der Holländer, die Holländerin*	*Holländisch*
Österreich (Austria)	*der Österreicher, die Österreicherin*	*Deutsch*
Russland	*der Russe, die Russin*	*Russisch*
Schweden (Sweden)	*der Schwede, die Schwedin*	*Schwedisch*
die Schweiz (Switzerland)	*der Schweizer, die Schweizerin*	*Deutsch Französisch, Italienisch*
Spanien (Spain)	*der Spanier, die Spanierin*	*Spanisch*

Das Land (country)	Die Nationalität (nationality)	Die Sprache (language)
die Türkei	der Türke, die Türkin	Türkisch
die USA (OO ESS AH) or die Vereinigten Staaten von Amerika (The United States [of America])	der Amerikaner, die Amerikanerin	Englisch

Some examples of how these words can be used in sentences are given below.

- *Sie kommen aus Deutschland.* They come from Germany.
- *Sie sind Deutsche.* They are Germans.
- *Sie sprechen Deutsch.* They speak German.
- *Verstehen Sie Deutsch?* Do you understand German?
- *Sind Sie Amerikaner? Nein, ich bin Deutscher.* Are you an American? No, I am German.
- *Er ist in Österreich.* He is in Austria.
- *Ich komme aus den Vereinigten Staaten.* I come from the United States.

When describing a nationality, you do not use the definite article: *Ich bin Amerikaner. Sie sind Spanierin.*

Days and Dates

The days of the week are all masculine nouns because they are compound words formed with the word *der Tag* (except for the word for Wednesday).

▶ Days of the Week

German	English
Sonntag	Sunday
Montag	Monday
Dienstag	Tuesday
Mittwoch	Wednesday
Donnerstag	Thursday
Freitag	Friday
Sonnabend/Samstag	Saturday

If you ask *Was ist heute?* (What is today?), the answer is one of the days of the week.

- *Was ist heute? Heute ist Montag.*
- *Was ist heute? Heute ist Freitag.*
- *Ist heute Montag oder Dienstag? Heute ist Montag.**
- *Ist heute Mittwoch oder Donnerstag? Heute ist Donnerstag.**

*oder = or

The days of the week are used in an adverbial phrase when preceded by the preposition *am* (contraction of *an dem*). Then they tell "when" something occurs.

- *Wann ist das Konzert* (concert)? *Das Konzert ist am Montag.*
- *Wann ist die Party? Die Party ist am Sonnabend.*
- *Wann kommt Herr Meyer? Herr Meyer kommt am Freitag.**
- *Wann gehst du nach Hause? Ich gehe am Donnerstag nach Hause.**

*kommt = comes; *gehst, gehe* = go

The Seasons of the Year

The German words for the seasons of the year are partially similar to the English words.

▶ **Seasons of the Year**

German	English
Sommer	summer
Herbst	fall
Winter	winter
Frühling	spring

And, like English, they are used very frequently with the preposition *in*. But in German, you have to say "in the" season and use the contraction *im: im Sommer, im Herbst, im Winter, im Frühling*.

If you begin a sentence with one of the seasons, remember to place the verb before the subject: *Im Winter sind wir in Florida*.

Glückwunsch

It's a mouthful, but that's how you say "happy birthday" in German. Naturally, it will be helpful to know the German months if you're going to talk about birthdays.

German months are very similar to their English counterparts.

▶ **Months of the Year**

German	English
Januar	January
Februar	February
März	March
April	April

German	English
Mai	May
Juni	June
Juli	July
August	August
September	September
Oktober	October
November	November
Dezember	December

They are used in exactly the same way as the English months: in January (*im Januar*), in May (*im Mai*), in September (*im September*). Notice, however, that German uses *im* (the contraction of *in dem*) in place of *in*.

To tell what month you were born in, just say: *Ich bin im Februar geboren.* (I was born in February.) *Ich bin im Juni geboren.* (I was born in June.) You can change the verb *sein* (to be) appropriately to say what month others were born in: *Vater ist im Oktober geboren.* (Father was born in October.) *Die Zwillinge sind im März geboren.* (The twins were born in March.) *Wann bist du geboren?* (When were you born?)

And if you want to say that something occurred in a certain year, you say *im Jahre: im Jahre 1776, im Jahre 2002. Ich bin im Jahre 1985 geboren.* (I was born in 1985.)

German years are said like this: 1985 = *neunzehnhundertfünfundachtzig.*

And if you want to tell in what month your birthday is, you say, *Ich habe im April Geburtstag.* (I have a birthday in April.) *Er hat im Juli Geburtstag.* (He has a birthday in July.)

Telling Time

The term *der Morgen* is a noun that means "morning." It is used in many expressions on telling time. Here are some important words to know to talk about time of day:

- *der Abend* (evening)
- *der Morgen* (morning)
- *die Nacht* (night)
- *der Tag* (day)

▶ **The Times of Day in German**

German Expression	English Expression
gestern Abend	yesterday evening
gestern Morgen	yesterday morning
gestern Nachmittag	yesterday afternoon
gestern Nacht	last night
heute Abend	this evening
heute Morgen	this morning
heute Nachmittag	this afternoon
heute Nacht	tonight
morgen Abend	tomorrow evening
morgen früh	tomorrow morning
morgen Nachmittag	tomorrow afternoon
morgen Nacht	tomorrow night
übermorgen	the day after tomorrow
vorgestern	the day before yesterday

*Don't confuse *Morgen,* the noun that means "morning," with *morgen,* the adverb that means "tomorrow."

Hours and Minutes

What if you need to be more specific than just "yesterday evening" or "this afternoon"? You'll need to use the clock to indicate a specific time. The word *die Uhr* means "the clock." But the same word is placed after time to mean "o'clock." There are a few kinds of clocks and watches in German, and they typically end with *Uhr* (note the exception in this list):

- *die Armbanduhr* (wristwatch)
- *die Taschenuhr* (pocket watch)
- *die Wanduhr* (wall clock)
- *der Wecker* (the alarm clock)

When time is on the hour, you merely say the number and follow it by *Uhr: ein Uhr* (one o'clock), *zwei Uhr* (two o'clock), *drei Uhr* (three o'clock), *sieben Uhr* (seven o'clock), *zwölf Uhr* (twelve o'clock), *dreizehn Uhr* (thirteen o'clock, or one o'clock p.m.), *achtzehn Uhr* (six o'clock p.m.), *zwanzig Uhr* (eight o'clock p.m.), *einundzwanzig Uhr* (nine o'clock p.m.), *zweiundzwanzig Uhr* (ten o'clock p.m.), *dreiundzwanzig Uhr* (eleven o'clock p.m.), *vierundzwanzig Uhr* (twelve midnight).

The times that occur between the top of the hour and the half hour all come *nach* (after):

1:10	*zehn nach eins*	(ten past one)
4:20	*zwanzig nach vier*	(twenty past four)
6:15	*Viertel nach sechs*	(a quarter past six)

If the time is thirty minutes after the hour, use the word *halb* (half) and the *next* hour. Think of it as being "halfway" to the next hour.

2:30	*halb drei*	(two-thirty)
9:30	*halb zehn*	(nine-thirty)

And if the times occur between the half hour and the three-quarter hour, use *nach* followed by the expression for the half hour:

3:35   *fünf Minuten nach halb vier* (five minutes past three-thirty, three thirty-five)

7:40   *zehn Minuten nach halb acht* (ten minutes past seven-thirty, six forty)

Germans often leave out the word *Minuten: zehn nach halb acht* (ten past seven-thirty. six forty).

From a quarter before the hour to the top of the next hour, use *vor* (before):

12:45   *Viertel vor eins* (a quarter to one)

4:50   *zehn Minuten vor fünf / zehn vor fünf* (ten to five)

Asking for the Time
To ask what time it is, use one of these expressions: *Wieviel Uhr ist es?* (What time is it?) or *Wie spät ist es?* (How late is it?). Some possible responses are:

- *Es ist halb zehn.* (It's nine-thirty.)
- *Es ist neunzehn Uhr.* (It's seven o'clock p.m.)
- *Es ist Viertel vor sieben.* (It's a quarter until seven.)
- *Es ist zwei Uhr.* (It's two o'clock.)

To ask "at" what time something occurs, precede the time by the preposition *um.* Note the use of *um* in these questions and answers.

▶ Using *um* When Telling Time

Question	Answer
Um wie viel Uhr kommt der Zug? (At what time does the train come?)	*Der Zug kommt um vierzehn Uhr.* (The train comes at two o'clock p.m.)
Um wie viel Uhr ist die Prüfung? (At what time is the exam?)	*Die Prüfung ist um halb neun.* (The exam is at eight-thirty.)
Um wie viel Uhr gehen Sie nach Hause? (At what time are you going home?)	*Ich gehe um elf Uhr nach Hause.* (I am going home at eleven o'clock.)

And just like English, German has special words for "noon" and "midnight": *Mittag* (literally: "midday") and *Mitternacht.* They are used in place of twelve o'clock:

- *Es ist jetzt zwölf Uhr.* (It is now twelve o'clock.)
- *Es ist jetzt Mittag.* (It is now noon.)
- *Er kommt um Mitternacht.* (He comes at midnight.)

Family Members

Did you know that German families have specialized words for family members just like American families do? You don't want to use the wrong word for a specific relationship. It would be just as much of a mistake in Germany as it would be in the United States to introduce your wife's mother as your "grandmother" instead of as your "mother-in-law."

So here's a German family tree. You'll see that it follows the same lines as an American family tree.

▶ Members of a German Family

German	English
der Urgroßvater	great-grandfather
die Urgroßmutter	great-grandmother
der Großvater	grandfather
der Opa	grandpa
die Großmutter	grandmother
die Oma	grandma
der Vater	father
der Vati	dad, daddy
die Mutter	mother
die Mutti	mom, mommy
der Stiefvater	stepfather
die Stiefmutter	stepmother
der Ehemann or *Mann*	husband
die Ehefrau or *Frau*	wife
der Sohn	son
die Tochter	daughter
der Stiefsohn	stepson
die Stieftochter	stepdaughter
der Stiefbruder	stepbrother
die Stiefschwester	stepsister
der Bruder	brother
die Schwester	sister
die Geschwister	brothers and sisters
der Enkel	grandson
die Enkelin	granddaughter
der Vetter (also: *Cousin*)	male cousin
die Kusine (also: *Cousine*)	female cousin

German	English
der Neffe	nephew
die Nichte	niece
der Onkel	uncle
German	*English*
die Tante	aunt
der Schwiegervater	father-in-law
die Schwiegermutter	mother-in-law
der Schwiegersohn	son-in-law
die Schwiegertochter	daughter-in-law
der Schwager	brother-in-law
die Schwägerin	sister-in-law
der Verlobte	fiancé
die Verlobte	fiancée
die Großeltern	grandparents
die Eltern	parents
die Schwiegereltern	in-laws
die Verwandten	relatives

Basic Food and Eating Terms

If you're visiting Germany or another German-speaking country, you're going to have to eat eventually. You need some information for getting around a restaurant and its menu.

First, you have to identify what's a restaurant and what isn't. There are many words that tell you that you've found an eatery:

▶ **Places to Eat**

German	English
der Biergarten	beer garden
die Bierhalle	beer hall
das Café	café

German	English
das Gasthaus	inn, tavern
der Gasthof	inn, tavern
die Gaststätte	inn, tavern
German	*English*
die Imbisshalle	snackbar
die Konditorei	pastry shop that serves snacks and beverages
die Mensa	cafeteria in a university
die Raststätte	roadside café
der Ratskeller	restaurant in the cellar of the town hall
das Restaurant	restaurant
der Schnellimbiss	snackbar
die Weinstube	wine café, serving light food

If you're looking for just a bite to eat, look for a name with *Café* or *Gaststätte* in it. For a full meal, you'll probably want a *Restaurant* or *Ratskeller*.

Der Ratskeller is usually found in the cellar of the town hall, called *das Rathaus.* You can get full meals there and a wide selection of wines.

Just as in the United States, ethnic food is very popular in Germany. There are many American-style fast-food places, including some that are actually transplants from the United States: McDonald's, Burger King, KFC, and so on.

Restaurant names vary as much in Germany as here. The owner's name might identify the place. Or a city. Or an animal. Or some trendy phrase. When you see a name like *Café Madrid,* it's not hard to figure out where the name came from. But it's common to begin the name of an inn or other eating establishment with *zu.* The preposition *zu,* if you look it up in a dictionary, basically means "to." But when it's used with the name of an inn, you should think of it as meaning *The Inn of . . .* : *Zum roten*

Löwen (The Inn of the Red Lion), *Zur alten Mühle* (The Old Mill Inn).

You can easily learn the German names of food, beverages, and utensils. Some of the primary ones are given below.

▶ Food

German	English Foods
die Birne	pear
die Bratwurst	roasted sausage
der Brokkoli	broccoli
die Erbsen	peas
die Erdbeeren	strawberries
der Fisch	fish
das Hähnchen	chicken
die Kartoffeln	potatoes
der Käse	cheese
der Kohl	cabbage
die Möhren	carrots
das Obst	fruit
die Pilze	mushrooms
der Reis	rice
das Rindfleisch	beef
das Sauerkraut	sauerkraut
der Schinken	ham
das Schweinefleisch	pork
der Speck	bacon
der Spinat	spinach
die Zwiebeln	onions

▶ Beverages

German	English
das Bier	beer
der Kaffee	coffee
die Milch	milk
das Pils	lager beer
der Rotwein, Weißwein	red wine, white wine
der Tee	tea
das Wasser	water
der Wein	wine

▶ Utensils

German	English
die Flasche	bottle
die Gabel	fork
das Glas	glass
der Löffel	spoon
das Messer	knife
die Serviette	napkin
der Suppenteller	soup bowl (plate)
die Tasse	cup
der Teller	plate

03 / Grammar

Intro to Grammar
English and German are Germanic languages and are derived from the same Indo-European source. It is that legacy of language that still exists in modern English that makes learning German a relatively easy task.

Understanding Gender
In the English language, "gender" refers to the sex of living things: Males are of the masculine gender and females are of the feminine gender. Inanimate objects are called neuter. German is a bit different.

The German Concept of Gender:
In general, German looks at words that represent males as masculine and words that represent females as feminine. But gender is not entirely based on sex. It is related to how a word is formed, rather than the sexual gender involved.

Der is used frequently with males: *der Vater, der Professor, der Student. Die* is used frequently with females*: die Mutter, die Frau, die Tante* (aunt). But that's where it ends, because the three genders, denoted by the articles *der, die,* and *das,* depend more on word formation than anything else to determine what is masculine, feminine, or neuter.

English speakers must clear their minds of the idea that gender is strictly sexual and animate or inanimate. When you speak German, you must accept the idea that masculine nouns, which use *der* as their definite article, do not necessarily refer to males. Likewise, feminine nouns, which use *die* as their definite article, do not always refer to females. And neuter nouns, which use *das* as their definite article, do not refer exclusively to inanimate objects.

Person, Place, or Thing?

In many German language textbooks, students are told that they must simply memorize the gender of each noun. That's not very efficient, and that's certainly not what Germans do. As they grow up with their language, German children hear the patterns of words that require a certain gender and gradually conform to them. Along the way, they memorize the exceptions. Identifying the patterns is very helpful in determining gender, and it eliminates the need for a great deal of memorization.

There are some broad rules for determining which gender a noun is. And it should be admitted early that in many cases there will be exceptions to the rules. But the rules are helpful guideposts for making intelligent choices when using *der, die,* or *das.*

Here are four basic categories of masculine nouns.
(There are more than just four, but these are a good start-
ing point.) Many—but not all—words that end in *–er, –el,*
or *–en* tend to be masculine. In addition, cognates that
refer to men also tend to be masculine. Take a look at
some examples.

▶ **Determining the Gender of Masculine Nouns**

Nouns Ending in –er	Nouns Ending in –el	Nouns Ending in –en	Cognates
der Vater	der Onkel (uncle)	der Laden (store, shop)	der Professor
der Lehrer (teacher)	der Löffel (spoon)	der Wagen (car)	der Diplomat
der Keller (cellar)	der Sattel (saddle)	der Magen (stomach)	der Tourist

Notice that half of the words listed above are inanimate objects. But all are masculine.

Additionally, nouns ending in *–ling* are always
masculine.

- *der Frühling* (spring)
- *der Neuling* (novice, beginner)
- *der Sperling* (sparrow)

Nouns ending in *–ig* and *–ich* are masculine.
- *der König* (king)
- *der Teppich* (rug, carpet)

Many words of one syllable that end in a consonant
are masculine.

- *der Arzt* (doctor)
- *der Brief* (letter)
- *der Stuhl* (chair)
- *der Bus* (bus)
- *der Tag* (day)
- *der Film* (film)
- *der Tisch* (table)
- *der Freund* (male friend)
- *der Wein* (wine)
- *der Markt* (market)
- *der Zug* (train)
- *der Park* (park)
- *der Platz* (market square, place, theater seat)

The Feminine Nouns

There are categories of feminine nouns that will help you determine the feminine gender. Words that refer exclusively to women are usually (but not always) feminine. Words that refer to women and inanimate objects ending in *–e* tend to be feminine. Words ending in *–in* are feminine. Words that end in *–ung* are feminine. Look at these examples:

▶ **Determining the Gender of Feminine Nouns**

Words Referring to Women	Words Ending in –e	Words Ending in –in	Words Ending in –ung
die Mutter	die Tante	die Studentin	die Prüfung (test)
die Schwester (sister)	die Tasse (cup)	die Lehrerin (female teacher)	die Übung (exercise)
die Frau	die Schule (school)	die Freundin (girlfriend)	die Achtung (attention)

Notice how many of these words are inanimate objects. Yet they are all feminine.

Feminine nouns ending in *–in* usually have a masculine counterpart that does not have that ending. The two forms distinguish males and females having the same role. Here are some examples:

▶ **Gendered Roles**

The Male Role	*The Female Role*
der Arzt (physician)	*die Ärztin* (physician)
der Freund (boyfriend)	*die Freundin* (girlfriend)
der Künstler (artist)	*die Künstlerin* (artist)
der Sänger (singer)	*die Sängerin* (singer)
der Schüler (pupil)	*die Schülerin* (pupil)

Additionally, nouns ending in *–schaft* are always feminine.

- *die Botschaft* (message, embassy)
- *die Wirtschaft* (economy)
- *die Freundschaft* (friendship)
- *die Wissenschaft* (science)
- *die Landschaft* (landscape)

Words that end in *–ei* are feminine:
- *die Bäckerei* (bakery)
- *die Konditorei* (confectioner)
- *die Metzgerei* (butcher's shop)

Words that end in *–tät* are feminine:
- *die Qualität* (quality)
- *die Universität* (university)

Nouns ending in *–heit, –keit,* and *–ie* are always feminine:

- *die Einsamkeit* (loneliness)
- *die Gesundheit* (health)
- *die Poesie* (poetry)

Both German and English have inherited a large number of words that end in *–tion.* In German they are always feminine, and they usually have the same meaning as their English counterpart. But the German pronunciation of *–tion* is different from English: *Position* (poh-zee-tsee-OHN), *Situation* (zit-oo-ah-tsee-OHN). Look at the following words:

- *die Formation*
- *die Information*
- *die Inspektion*
- *die Koalition*
- *die Konstitution*
- *die Position*
- *die Reservation*
- *die Revolution*
- *die Situation*
- *die Ventilation*
- *die Vibration*

The Neuter Nouns

Let's start with a reminder: Not all inanimate nouns in German are neuter (*das*). There are patterns to watch for when deciding whether a noun is neuter. Diminutives are always neuter. They end either in *–chen* or *–lein.* Words that end in *–um* or *–ium* are always neuter. Words that begin with the prefix *Ge–* tend to be neuter. Look at these examples:

▶ **Neuter Nouns**

Diminutive with *–chen or –lein*	*Ending –um or –ium*	*Prefix* Ge–
das Mädchen (girl)	*das Datum* (date)	*das Gemüse* (vegetables)
das Fräulein (young lady)	*das Studium* (study)	*das Getreide* (grain)
das Brötchen (bread roll)	*das Gymnasium* (prep school)	*das Gespenst* (ghost)

Note that some of these neuter words refer to people rather than to inanimate objects.

Another category of neuter nouns is infinitives that are used as nouns. These are always neuter.

- *das Einkommen* (income)
- *das Singen* (singing)
- *das Schreiben* (writing)
- *das Essen* (food)
- *das Tanzen* (dancing)

Certain categories of words tend to be of one gender. Take note of how the following words are related and of their gender.

▶ **A Category of Words That Share the Same Gender—** *Das Metall* (Metal)

English	*German*
aluminum	*das Aluminium*
brass	*das Messing*

English	German
gold	*das Gold*
iron	*das Eisen*
lead	*das Blei*
silver	*das Silber*
tin	*das Zinn*

German wouldn't be German without an exception. The metals have one, too: *der Stahl* (steel).

Exceptions to the Gender Patterns

Since there are exceptions in the various patterns, here are just a few to consider:

- *das Bett* (bed)
- *das Bier* (beer)
- *das Brot* (bread)
- *die Fabel* (fable)
- *das Fahrrad* (bike)
- *das Flugzeug* (airplane)
- *der Franzose* (Frenchman)
- *der Geschmack* (taste)
- *das Glas* (glass)
- *das Kind* (child)
- *das Konzert* (concert)
- *der Junge* (boy)
- *die Schwester* (sister)
- *die Tochter* (daughter)
- *das Wasser* (water)
- *das Wetter* (weather)
- *das Wochenende* (weekend)
- *die Wurst* (sausage)

You've learned that many words that end in *–e* are feminine: *die Dame* (lady), *die Tasse* (cup), *die Lampe* (lamp), and so on. But there are several masculine words that end in *–e,* too. Memorize these so you can remember that they don't follow the rule.

▶ **Masculine Nouns Ending in *–e***

German Noun	English Meaning
der Alte	old man
der Buchstabe	letter (of the alphabet)
der Franzose	Frenchman
der Hase	hare
der Junge	boy
der Knabe	boy, lad
der Löwe	lion
der Matrose	sailor
der Name	name
der Neffe	nephew
der Ochse	ox

Exceptions to the rules, like those words listed above, will always exist. With these words, there is no getting around memorizing their gender when you learn the noun.

In German, the articles and indefinite articles that you learned here are called the nominative case. This simply means that these nouns are acting as the subjects of sentences.

Articles Are Important

Just like English, German has definite and indefinite articles. Definite articles refer to specific persons or things (the man, the woman, the child), and indefinite articles refer to unspecific persons or things (a man, a woman, a child).

The articles you have learned so far are the definite articles. Let's review them.

▶ Definite Articles and Gender

Masculine	Feminine	Neuter	English Meaning
der	die	das	the

The gender patterns that you encountered earlier in this chapter work the same with indefinite articles. But the good news is that you only have to keep your eye on feminine nouns when choosing the indefinite article. Masculine and neuter nouns have the same form: *ein.* The feminine indefinite article is *eine.*

▶ Indefinite Articles and Gender

Masculine	Feminine	Neuter	English Meaning
ein	eine	ein	a / an

Look at these examples to see how they relate to the definite articles:

▶ Comparing the Indefinite and Definite Articles

Masculine Nouns	Feminine Nouns	Neuter Nouns
der Mann / ein Mann	die Frau / eine Frau	das Kind / ein Kind
der Laden / ein Laden	die Klasse / eine Klasse	das Studium / ein Studium
der Onkel / ein Onkel	die Freundin / eine Freundin	das Geschenk / ein Geschenk

Making Nouns Plural

So you understand articles and that all nouns have gender. But what about when there are more than one of something? In this section you'll learn how to talk about men, women, cars, books, and anything else you can have two or more of, plus you'll learn how to use pronouns so you don't have to keep repeating yourself.

Several German nouns are identical in both the singular and plural. You can tell when the noun is plural only by the verb used with it or by a number preceding it. Look at these examples:

- *ein Brunnen ist . . .*   a well is . . .
- *zehn Brunnen sind . . .*   ten wells are . . .
- *ein Mädchen ist . . .*   a girl is . . .
- *zehn Mädchen sind . . .*   ten girls are . . .
- *ein Schauspieler ist . . .*   an actor is . . .
- *zehn Schauspieler sind . . .*   ten actors are . . .

When a noun is plural, it uses *die* as its definite article, no matter what its gender. Very few German nouns form their plural by adding an *–s,* though a few do follow that pattern. See the following table for some examples.

▶ **Making a Noun Plural by Adding an** *–s*

Singular Noun	Plural Noun
der Park (park)	*die Parks* (parks)
das Foto (photo)	*die Fotos* (photos)
die Kamera (camera)	*die Kameras* (cameras)

This is the simplest way that plurals may be formed, but it is not the typical way. Most plurals are formed in other ways, similar to irregular plurals in English, such as child/children, mouse/mice, goose/geese.

The Plural of Masculine Nouns

Masculine nouns that end in *–er, –el,* or *–en* have no ending in the plural, but they may require adding an Umlaut. Some examples with masculine nouns are shown in the following table.

▶ **Plural of Masculine Nouns Ending in *–er, –el,* or *–en***

Singular Noun	Plural Noun with Numbers	Plural Noun with Definite Article
der Schauspieler (the actor)	sechs Schauspieler (six actors)	die Schauspieler (the actors)
der Löffel (the spoon)	zwei Löffel (two spoons)	die Löffel (the spoons)
der Laden (the shop)	acht Läden (eight shops)	die Läden (the shops)
der Vater (the father)	drei Väter (three fathers)	die Väter (the fathers)

Note how *Laden* and *Vater* have added an Umlaut above the *a* in the plural form.

Other masculine nouns, particularly short, one-syllable nouns, usually form their plural by adding *–e* to the noun. Often an Umlaut is required.

▶ **Masculine Plural Ending −e**

Singular Noun	Plural Noun with Numbers	Plural Noun with Definite Article
der Abend (the evening)	zwei Abende (two evenings)	die Abende (the evenings)
der Brief (the letter)	sechs Briefe (six letters)	die Briefe (the letters)
der Bus (the bus)	zwei Busse (two buses)	die Busse (the buses)
der Markt (the market)	drei Märkte (three markets)	die Märkte (the markets)
der Sohn (the son)	vier Söhne (four sons)	die Söhne (the sons)
der Stuhl (the chair)	vier Stühle (four chairs)	die Stühle (the chairs)
der Tag (the day)	zehn Tage (ten days)	die Tage (the days)
der Zug (the train)	acht Züge (eight trains)	die Züge (the trains)

One high-frequency masculine noun that doesn't follow these patterns is *der Mann* (man). It forms its plural by adding an Umlaut and the ending *−er: zwei Männer* (two men), *die Männer* (the men).

Feminine Nouns in the Plural

Just like masculine nouns, feminine nouns don't change to the plural by simply adding an *−s*. Most feminine nouns change to the plural by adding *−n* or *−en*. And just like all other plural nouns, they use *die* as the definite article.

▶ Forming Plurals of Feminine Nouns by Adding *−n* or *−en*

Singular	Plural
die Frau (the woman)	*die Frauen* (the women)
die Schwester (the sister)	*die Schwestern* (the sisters)
die Straße (the street)	*die Straßen* (the streets)
die Tasse (the cup)	*die Tassen* (the cups)

If a feminine noun ends in *−in,* the plural ending is *−nen. Die Freundin* (girlfriend) becomes *die Freundinnen* (girlfriends).

There are two notable exceptions to the rule regarding *−n* or *−en* for feminine nouns. Note that the only change in these two words is the addition of an Umlaut in the plural:

- *die Mutter* (mother) / *die Mütter* (mothers)
- *die Tochter* (daughter) / *die Töchter* (daughters)

Making Neuter Nouns Plural

Many neuter words follow a similar pattern to some masculine words: There is no ending change in the plural. Examples:

▶ Neuter Plural Formation for Nouns That Take No Ending

Singular	Plural
das Fenster (the window)	*die Fenster* (the windows)
das Klassenzimmer (the classroom)	*die Klassenzimmer* (the classrooms)
das Mädchen (the girl)	*die Mädchen* (the girls)

Neuter words, particularly those of one syllable, tend to form their plural by the ending *−er.* An Umlaut may also be added in some cases.

▶ **Neuter Plural Formation for Nouns That Take an –er Ending**

Singular	Plural
das Fahrrad (the bicycle)	die Fahrräder (the bicycles)
das Glas (the glass)	die Gläser (the glasses)
das Haus (the house)	die Häuser (the houses)
das Kind (the child)	die Kinder (the children)
das Land (the country)	die Länder (the countries)

Words that end in –chen and –lein change just the article from das to die; no endings are added. Das Mädchen (the girl) becomes die Mädchen (the girls), das Röslein (the little rose) becomes die Röslein (the little roses).

Be aware that these rules regarding plural formations show only a tendency. They are meant to help guide you. But there will always be exceptions. Using German plurals accurately will come with experience and time.

Pronouns

Now that you have a feeling for German gender, it's time to meet the pronouns that go along with the gender of nouns. Pronouns are words that take the place of a noun. They follow the patterns you have already learned with nouns. Interestingly, the German pronouns for "he," "she," and "it" resemble very much the definite articles.

▶ **Third Person Singular Pronouns**

Gender	Definite Article	Pronoun
masculine	der	er (he or it)
feminine	die	sie (she or it)
neuter	das	es (he, she, or it)

Remember that German gender is not based on sexual gender. That's why *er* means both "he" and "it," and *sie* means both "she" and "it." It depends on the meaning of the noun. Look at these examples:

▶ Pronoun Substitution

Noun Subject	Pronoun Replacement	Translation
Der Mann ist da.	*Er ist da.*	He is there.
Der Mantel ist da.	*Er ist da.*	It is there.
Die Studentin ist in der Stadt.	*Sie ist in der Stadt.*	She is in the city.
Die Schule ist in der Stadt.	*Sie ist in der Stadt.*	It is in the city.
Das Kind ist hier.	*Es ist hier.*	He/she is here.
Das Geschenk ist hier.	*Es ist hier.*	It is here.

You and I

In addition to the third person pronouns that you just learned, you should know the first and second person personal pronouns.

▶ Personal Pronouns—Singular

Person	English Pronoun	German Pronoun
First	I	*ich*
Second	you	*du* (informal), *Sie* (formal)
Third	he, she, it	*er, sie, es*

Sie is the formal way to say "you," which you would use with anyone you don't know or anyone older than you or in a position of authority. There's no exact English equivalent. It is always capitalized. And don't let the word for "she" or "it" (*sie*) confuse you, even though it looks the same—it's always spelled with a lowercase letter except at the beginning of a sentence.

The German word for the pronoun "I" is *ich* and is never capitalized except at the beginning of a sentence. It's just the opposite of English.

Plural Pronouns

To talk about nouns that are plural without repeating them over and over, you'll need to use the plural pronouns.

▶ Personal Pronouns—Plural

Person	English Pronoun	German Pronoun
First	we	*wir*
Second	you all	*ihr*
Third	they	*sie*

Here are some examples:

- *Vater und Mutter* becomes *sie* (pl.)
- *Benno und Ilse* becomes *sie* (pl.)
- *Karl und ich* becomes *wir*
- *der Schüler und ich* becomes *wir*

Using You

German has three different pronouns that mean "you," as you have now seen. German has a plural, informal pronoun (the plural of *du*). It is *ihr.* Yes, it also means "you." And, of course, you've already encountered *Sie,* which is the formal pronoun "you." So let's look at those forms of "you" again and put them in perspective.

- *du* (you, sing.)   used to address one person on an informal or familiar basis
- *ihr* (you, pl.)   used to address more than one person on an informal or familiar basis
- *Sie* (you, sing. or pl.) used to address one or more persons on a formal basis

"Informal" here means that the person to whom you are speaking is a relative or a close friend and you are on a first-name basis with one another. "Formal" here means that the person to whom you are speaking is older, in a position of respect or authority, or is someone you don't know well. You use a title and a last name when addressing this person: *Herr Braun, Professor Brenner, Doktor Schmidt.*

Adjectives and Where They Stand

Just like English adjectives, German adjectives can stand alone at the end of a phrase to describe a noun in a sentence. These adjectives are called predicate adjectives.

- The child is little. *Das Kind ist klein.*
- Uncle Jack is young. *Onkel Hans ist jung.*
- Grandmother gets furious. *Großmutter wird wütend.*

In this regard, German and English adjectives are used in the very same way. But when an adjective stands directly in front of a noun, that's where English and German differ. German adjectives add an ending when they stand in front of a noun.

- The little child is sad. *Das kleine Kind ist traurig.*
- The young man is playing soccer. *Der junge Mann spielt Fußball.*
- The old lady likes it. *Die alte Dame hat es gern.*

When using the definite article (*der, die, das*) with a singular noun, the adjective ending is *–e.* But if the noun is plural, the ending is *–en.*

- *Das kleine Kind ist traurig. Die kleinen Kinder sind traurig.*
- *Der junge Mann spielt Fußball. Die jungen Männer spielen Fußball.*
- *Die alte Dame hat es gern. Die alten Damen haben es gern.*

▶ Adjectives

German	English
arm	poor
kurz	short
blau	blue
lang	long
braun	brown
langweilig	boring
gelb	yellow
neu	new
grau	gray
reich	rich
grün	green
rot	red

German	English
hässlich	ugly
schwarz	black
hübsch	beautiful/handsome
weiß	white
interessant	interesting

Here are some examples of predicate adjectives (which take no endings) compared to adjectives in front of the nouns they modify (which do take endings).

- *Die Lehrerin ist alt.* (The teacher is old.)
- *die alte Lehrerin* (the old teacher)
- *Das Kind ist klein.* (The child is small.)
- *das kleine Kind* (the small child)
- *Die Kinder sind traurig.* (The children are sad.)
- *die traurigen Kinder* (the sad children)
- *Die Frauen sind hübsch.* (The women are beautiful.)
- *die hübschen Frauen* (the beautiful women)
- *Die Vase ist grün.* (The vase is green.)
- *die grüne Vase* (the green vase)

Verbs: Infinitives, Auxiliaries, and Conjugations

A verb is one of the most important elements of any language. They tell what's going on: singing, running, fighting, crying, sleeping, drinking, talking, loving, and . . . on and on. Here you'll learn how to conjugate verbs and form sentences. Before long, you'll be speaking like a native!

Conjugate What?

Infinitives, in any language, are the basic form of verbs. In English, infinitives begin with the word "to" and look like this: to run, to jump, to follow, to argue, to be. In German they end in *–n* or *–en: sein, gehen, heißen.*

Conjugating a verb means to put the appropriate endings on the verb that correspond to the various pronouns. In English that's a relatively simple matter. You drop the word "to" from the infinitive and add an *–s* to the third person singular (he, she, it). Look at the example here.

▶ Verb Endings in English

Pronoun	to run	to speak	to be	to understand
I	run	speak	am	understand
you	run	speak	are	understand
he, she, it	runs	speaks	is	understands
we	run	speak	are	understand
they	run	speak	are	understand

When it comes to verbs, English is a little more complicated than German. Watch out for the two present tense forms that we have in English. German has only one. And both English forms are translated into German the same way. Look at these examples:

- I buy a house. *Ich kaufe ein Haus.*
- I am buying a house. *Ich kaufe ein Haus.*
- He goes home. *Er geht nach Hause.*
- He is going home. *Er geht nach Hause.*

The German Verb

You have already learned a bit about one of the most important verbs in German: *sein.* That's the infinitive form of the verb "to be."

▶ **Conjugating *sein* (to be)**

Person	English Conjugation	German Conjugation
First (sing.)	I am	*ich bin*
Second (sing.)	you are (informal)	*du bist*
Third (sing.)	he is, she is, it is	*er ist, sie ist, es ist*
First (pl.)	we are	*wir sind*
Second (pl.)	you are	*ihr seid*
Second (sing., pl.)	you are (formal)	*Sie sind*
Third (pl.)	they are	*sie sind*

You probably have noticed that there are three pronouns in German that look an awfully lot alike: *sie* (she), *Sie* (you formal), *sie* (they). Germans have no problem distinguishing these pronouns, because their usage is so specific. For one thing, *sie ist* can mean only "she is," because the verb *ist* is used only with *er, sie* (she), and *es*. And the context of a conversation would make clear whether *Sie* (you formal) or *sie* (they) is meant.

In this book, you will know that "you" is the meaning of *Sie* when you see it with a capitalized *S*. The other two forms will be identified as singular and plural. If you see *sie* (sing.), you will know that it means "she." If you see *sie* (pl.), you will know it means "they."

Going Somewhere? Verbs of Motion

It's time to start moving around a little more. Let's look at four verbs that are called verbs of motion. They describe how you get from one place to another: *gehen* (GAY-EN), to go on foot; *kommen* (KAW-men), to come; *fliegen* (FLEE-gen), to fly; and *fahren* (FAHR-en), to drive or to go by transportation.

They're used almost in the same way that their English counterparts are used, except that German tends to be a little more specific. In English we say, "I go to school." We don't tell whether we walk there, drive there, or fly there. In German there's a tendency to specify the means of conveyance: walking, driving, or flying.

To learn how to conjugate these verbs, you need to know the term "verb stem." A verb stem is the part of the infinitive remaining when you drop the final *–en: fahren/fahr, gehen/geh,* and so on. You add endings to the verb stem to conjugate each verb according to the person and number (singular or plural). Take a look at the following table.

▶ **Conjugational Endings of Verbs**

Person	Ending to Add to Verb Stem	Example
First (sing.)	*–e*	*ich gehe*
Second (sing.)	*–st*	*du gehst*
Third (sing.)	*–t*	*er, sie, es geht*
First (pl.)	*–en*	*wir gehen*
Second (pl.)	*–t*	*ihr geht*
Second formal (sing. or pl.)	*–en*	*Sie gehen*
Third (pl.)	*–en*	*sie gehen*

Now let's look at the conjugations of these verbs of motion.

▶ **Conjugating Verbs of Motion**

gehen	kommen	fliegen	fahren
ich gehe	*ich komme*	*ich fliege*	*ich fahre*
du gehst	*du kommst*	*du fliegst*	*du fährst*
er/sie/es geht	*er/sie/es kommt*	*er/sie/es fliegt*	*er/sie/es fährt*
wir gehen	*wir kommen*	*wir fliegen*	*wir fahren*
ihr geht	*ihr kommt*	*ihr fliegt*	*ihr fahrt*
Sie gehen	*Sie kommen*	*Sie fliegen*	*Sie fahren*
sie (pl.) gehen	*sie kommen*	*sie fliegen*	*sie fahren*

Notice that the second person singular and third person singular (*du, er, sie, es*) add an Umlaut in their conjugation of the verb *fahren: du fährst, er fährt, sie fährt, es fährt.* This is called a stem change.

Let's look at some examples of ways to use these verbs.

- *Ihr kommt aus Berlin.* (You all come from Berlin.)
- *Wir fliegen nach Hause.* (We fly home.)
- *Er fährt mit dem Bus.* (He goes [drives] by bus.)
- *Ich gehe mit Hans.* (I go with Hans.)
- *Sie fahren mit dem Zug.* (They are going by train.)

The phrase *kommen aus* is used regularly to tell what city, locale, or country you come from: *Ich komme aus Hamburg. Er kommt aus Bayern* (Bavaria). *Wir kommen aus Amerika.*

Essentials for Life: Eating and Drinking

Essen (ESS-en) (to eat) and *trinken* (TRIN-ken) (to drink) are not verbs of motion. But notice that their conjugation follows the same pattern as the other verbs you have learned.

Take note that the verb *essen*, like *fahren*, requires a slight change in the second and third person singular (*du, er, sie, es*): *du isst, er isst, sie isst, es isst.*

▶ **Conjugating *essen* and *trinken***

essen	trinken
ich esse	*ich trinke*
du isst	*du trinkst*
er/sie/es isst	*er/sie/es trinkt*
Sie essen	*Sie trinken*

essen	trinken
wir essen	*wir trinken*
ihr esst	*ihr trinkt*
sie (pl.) *essen*	*sie trinken*

Present Tense

Now that you know how to put the correct endings on German verbs, it's time to start collecting some useful ones to add to your vocabulary.

▶ Present Tense Conjugations of Some New Verbs

English	German infinitive	ich	du	er/sie/es	wir	ihr	Sie/sie (pl.)
to laugh	*lachen*	*lache*	*lachst*	*lacht*	*lachen*	*lacht*	*lachen*
to live	*leben*	*lebe*	*lebst*	*lebt*	*leben*	*lebt*	*leben*
to reside	*wohnen*	*wohne*	*wohnst*	*wohnt*	*wohnen*	*wohnt*	*wohnen*
to love	*lieben*	*liebe*	*liebst*	*liebt*	*lieben*	*liebt*	*lieben*
to need	*brauchen*	*brauche*	*brauchst*	*braucht*	*brauchen*	*braucht*	*brauchen*
to play	*spielen*	*spiele*	*spielst*	*spielt*	*spielen*	*spielt*	*spielen*
to say	*sagen*	*sage*	*sagst*	*sagt*	*sagen*	*sagt*	*sagen*
to seek	*suchen*	*suche*	*suchst*	*sucht*	*suchen*	*sucht*	*suchen*
to think	*denken*	*denke*	*denkst*	*denkt*	*denken*	*denkt*	*denken*
to visit	*besuchen*	*besuche*	*besuchst*	*besucht*	*besuchen*	*besucht*	*besuchen*

Watch out for *leben* and *wohnen.* The former means "to live, to be alive." The latter means "to live or reside" somewhere. *Andreas lebt wie ein König.* (Andreas lives like a king.) *Andreas wohnt jetzt in Berlin.* (Andreas is living in Berlin now.)

Below are five more new verbs to add to your German vocabulary. But they have a variation in the verb stem that you'll have to watch for.

If a German verb stem ends in *–d* or *–t,* you have to add an extra *–e* before adding a *–t* or an *–st* ending. This makes the conjugated verb easier to pronounce. You'll remember that the *–t* ending is needed after *er, sie, es,* and *ihr* and *–st* is used after *du.* Look at these examples:

▶ **Verb Stems Ending in** *–t* **or** *–d*

English	German infinitive	ich	du
to answer	*antworten*	*antworte*	*antwortest*
to find	*finden*	*finde*	*findest*
to send	*senden*	*sende*	*sendest*
to wait	*warten*	*warte*	*wartest*
to work	*arbeiten*	*arbeite*	*arbeitest*

English	German infinitive	er/sie/es	wir	ihr	Sie/sie (pl.)
to answer	*antworten*	*antwortet*	*antworten*	*antwortet*	*antworten*
to find	*finden*	*findet*	*finden*	*findet*	*finden*
to send	*senden*	*sendet*	*senden*	*sendet*	*senden*
to wait	*warten*	*wartet*	*warten*	*wartet*	*warten*
to work	*arbeiten*	*arbeitet*	*arbeiten*	*arbeitet*	*arbeiten*

Verbs That End in *-ieren*

There are numerous patterns of words that help to build a vocabulary rapidly. Another pattern is the verb ending *–ieren.* Verbs that have this ending tend to be very similar to English. And they're all regular verbs, so they don't require a change to the stem in conjugations.

Here are some useful words to learn:

- *akzeptieren* (to accept)
- *arrangieren* (to arrange)
- *diskutieren* (to discuss)
- *isolieren* (to isolate)
- *konfiszieren* (to confiscate)
- *kontrollieren* (to control, supervise)
- *kritisieren* (to criticize)
- *marschieren* (to march)
- *fotografieren* (to photograph)
- *reduzieren* (to reduce)
- *reparieren* (to repair)
- *reservieren* (to reserve)
- *riskieren* (to risk)
- *studieren* (to study)

A Very Versatile Verb

The word *bitten* is one of the most frequently used German words. It has more than just one meaning, of course.

Bitten means "to ask, to request" or "to beg." But it doesn't have anything to do with asking questions. It refers to asking someone to do something: "He asks her to remove her hat." "The teacher asks the class to remain very quiet."

- *Er bittet sie, stehen zu bleiben.* (He asks them to remain standing.)
- *Ich bitte ihn, nach Hause zu kommen.* (I ask him to come home.)

In addition, you will often hear the word when you walk up to a salesperson in a store. *"Bitte,"* the salesperson will say cheerfully. Or, *"Bitte schön."* It's comparable to "May I help you?" in English.

When the salesperson hands you your purchase, he or she might also say, *"Bitte schön."* In this case it means something like "here you are" or "here's your package."

And when you thank the salesperson (*danke schön*), the response will be *"bitte schön"* or *"bitte sehr"* (you're welcome).

Negation

To negate a sentence in German, you can use the word *nicht* (not). The word *nicht* comes after the verb.

- *Ich bin nicht Peter.* (I am not Peter.)
- *Er wohnt nicht in München.* (He does not live in Munich.)
- *Sie studiert nicht französisch.* (She is not studying French.)

However, if you use a sentence that uses the indefinite article *ein,* you can't use *nicht.* To negate *ein,* you use the word *kein* (KINE), which means "not any" or "no." *Kein* always replaces *ein.*

- *Ich habe kein Geld.* (I don't have any money.)
- *Ich habe keinen Teller.* (I have no plate.)

The same endings that you learned to use with *ein* must also be used with *kein.* You'll learn more about the endings that *ein*-words can take in the next chapter.

▶ Negating *ein* in the Genders

Masculine	Feminine	Neuter	English meaning
kein	*keine*	*kein*	not a/not any

- *Sie sehen eine Brücke. Sie sehen keine Brücke.* (They see a bridge. They don't see a bridge.)
- *Ich kaufe einen Teller. Ich kaufe keinen Teller.* (I buy a plate. I don't buy a plate.)

Irregular Verbs

Now that you've learned the basics about German verbs, it's time to look more closely at some verbs that take stem changes in the present tense. One of the most often used is the verb "to have." This section will also cover using the present tense to talk about the future.

The German Verb

One very common German verb is "to have"—*haben*. This verb, like some that you already learned, doesn't follow the rules of conjugation exactly. In the second and third person singular, the stem of the verb (the part left after you drop the *–en*) changes. It's time to become acquainted with the little irregularities found in this verb.

▶ Conjugating *haben* (to have)

Person	English Conjugation	German Conjugation
First (sing.)	I have	*ich habe*
Second (sing.)	you have	*du hast*
Third (sing.)	he/she/it has	*er/sie/es hat*
First (pl.)	we have	*wir haben*
Second (pl.)	you all have	*ihr habt*
Second (formal)	you have	*Sie haben*
Third (pl.)	they have	*sie* (pl.) *haben*

Practice saying the conjugation of the verb and place it in your memory. It's a very important verb to know. And just like *sein,* you can use it in a sentence with *heute* to indicate the present tense.

■ *Maria hat ein Examen.* (Maria has an exam.)
■ *Heute haben wir eine Übung.* (We are having an exercise today.)
■ *Ich habe eine Klasse.* (I have a class.)
■ *Du hast es.* (You have it.)
■ *Er hat eine Prüfung.* (He has a test.)

Expressing Like with Haben

German has a special way of saying that a person likes someone or something. To express "like" in German, conjugate *haben,* say what it is you like, and follow the whole phrase with the word *gern.*

▶ Using *gern haben* to Express Like

Conjugate haben	Direct Object (what you like)	gern	English Meaning
Ich habe	Gemüse	gern.	I like vegetables.
Du hast	das Mädchen	gern.	You like the girl.
Wir haben	Musik	gern.	We like music.
Haben Sie	Karl oder Hans	gern?	Do you like Karl or Hans?

You can also use *gern* following other verbs to show that you like doing something:

■ *Ich esse gern Obst.* (I like eating fruit.)
■ *Er trinkt gern Bier.* (He likes drinking beer.)
■ *Wir singen gern.* (We like singing.)

This is a very common phrase and one you should put in your treasury of vocabulary.

The Word Morgen

Morgen means "tomorrow" and indicates that something is occurring in the future. It is an adverb that tells "when" something is occurring. But you can use the present tense of a verb and still mean the future. It's just like English. You can specify the time by "today" or "tomorrow" using only a present tense verb.

- Today he is in Germany.
- Tomorrow he is in Germany.

Look at some German examples:

- *Heute sind wir in Hamburg.* (We are in Hamburg today.)
- *Morgen sind wir in Hamburg.* (We are in Hamburg tomorrow.)
- *Heute habe ich eine Prüfung.* (I have a test today.)
- *Morgen habe ich eine Prüfung.* (I have a test tomorrow.)

You can also use the present tense to infer a future meaning using the verbs of motion that you learned earlier.

- *Heute kommt er ins Kino.* (He is coming to the movies today.)
- *Morgen kommt er ins Kino.* (He is coming to the movies tomorrow.)
- *Heute fliegen wir nach Hause.* (We are flying home today.)

■ *Morgen fliegen wir nach Hause.* (We are flying home tomorrow.)

Stem Changes in the Present Tense

You learned early that German has some special forms in the present tense. The verb *fahren,* for example, requires an Umlaut in the second person singular (*du*) and third person singular (*er, sie, es*): *ich fahre, du fährst, er fährt,* and so on.

Three other verbs you should know fall into the same category of special changes. But notice that each verb has its own peculiar way of changing. The verb *wissen* (to know) becomes a new form, the verb *sprechen* (to speak) changes the vowel *–e* to *–i,* and the verb *laufen* (to run) adds an Umlaut.

▶ **The Conjugation of** *wissen, sprechen,* **and** *laufen*

Pronoun	wissen	sprechen	laufen
ich	weiß	spreche	laufe
du	weißt	sprichst	läufst
er, sie, es	weiß	spricht	läuft
wir	wissen	sprechen	laufen
ihr	wisst	sprecht	lauft
Sie, sie (pl.)	wissen	sprechen	laufen

Be careful of the spelling of the conjugation of *wissen.* There is no ending on the stem of the verb *weiß* with the pronouns *ich, er, sie,* and *es.* And with the pronoun *du* you only add a *–t* to the stem *weiß* (*du weißt*).

There aren't many verbs that change their form the way *wissen* does. But there are lots of useful words that follow the pattern of *sprechen* and *laufen.* Many words that have an *e* in the verb stem, like *sprechen,* change that *e* to an *i* or *ie*. And words that have the vowel *a* in the stem often add an Umlaut, like *laufen*. But remember that these little changes only occur in the second person singular (*du*) and the third person singular (*er, sie, es*). Here are some examples.

▶ **Verbs That Change *e* to *i***

English	German Infinitive	Conjugation with		
		ich	du	er
to break	*brechen*	*ich breche*	*du brichst*	*er bricht*
to give	*geben*	*ich gebe*	*du gibst*	*er gibt*
to help	*helfen*	*ich helfe*	*du hilfst*	*er hilft*
to meet	*treffen*	*ich treffe*	*du triffst*	*er trifft*
to take	*nehmen*	*ich nehme*	*du nimmst*	*er nimmt*

▶ **Verbs That Change *e* to *ie***

English	German Infinitive	Conjugation with		
		ich	du	er
to read	*lesen*	*ich lese*	*du liest*	*er liest*
to see	*sehen*	*ich sehe*	*du siehst*	*er sieht*

▶ **Verbs That Change *a* to *ä***

English	German Infinitive	Conjugation with		
		ich	du	er
to bake	*backen*	*ich backe*	*du bäckst*	*er bäckt*
to sleep	*schlafen*	*ich schlafe*	*du schläfst*	*er schläft*
to fall	*fallen*	*ich falle*	*du fällst*	*er fällt*
to carry, wear	*tragen*	*ich trage*	*du trägst*	*er trägt*
to wash	*waschen*	*ich wasche*	*du wäschst*	*er wäscht*
to let	*lassen*	*ich lasse*	*du lässt*	*er lässt*
to catch	*fangen*	*ich fange*	*du fängst*	*er fängt*

The Many Uses of Werden

Werden is a frequently used verb in German. It means "to become" or "to get" (She becomes a doctor. It's getting warm).

Its conjugation follows the pattern you already know, with a slight variation in the second and third persons singular.

▶ Conjugating *werden* (to get/to become)

Person	English Conjugation	German Conjugation
First (sing.)	I get / I become	*ich werde*
Second (sing.)	you get / you become	*du wirst*
Third (sing.)	he/she/it gets / he/she/it becomes	*er/sie/es wird*
First (pl.)	we get / we become	*wir werden*
Second (pl.)	you all get / you all become	*ihr werdet*
Second (formal)	you get / you become	*Sie werden*
Third (pl.)	they get / they become	*sie werden*

Past Tense

In German, there are two types of past tense, regular and irregular. Don't let it worry you. Fortunately for you as an English speaker, you have the advantage of knowing very similar past tense patterns in your native language.

For now you're just going to concentrate on the regular past tense. In English, that's where you tack on the ending "–ed" to a verb, and it takes on a past tense meaning.

- he jumps   he jumped
- we look   we looked
- I travel   I traveled

Just think of all the English verbs there are that form their past tense by this simple method. The German method is just as easy. Just add *–te* to the stem of the verb and it becomes past tense.

▶ Forming the Past Tense

Infinitive	Verb Stem	Past Tense
spielen (to play)	*spiel*	*spielte*
fragen (to ask)	*frag*	*fragte*
suchen (to search)	*such*	*suchte*

If the stem of the verb ends in *–t* or *–d,* you have to add an extra *–e* before placing the past tense ending *–te* on the end of the stem:

■   *warten* (to wait)   *wart*   *wartete*

After you have formed the past tense (*spielte, fragte, suchte, wartete*), you're not quite done. As with all German verbs, the conjugational ending must still be added. But notice that the endings for *ich, er, sie,* and *es* are the same: *–te.* The past tense conjugation of regular verbs will look like the ones in the following table.

▶ Conjugating the Past Tense

Pronoun	spielen	fragen	warten
ich	*spielte*	*fragte*	*wartete*
du	*spieltest*	*fragtest*	*wartetest*
er, sie, es	*spielte*	*fragte*	*wartete*
wir	*spielten*	*fragten*	*warteten*
ihr	*spieltet*	*fragtet*	*wartetet*
Sie	*spielten*	*fragten*	*warteten*
sie (pl.)	*spielten*	*fragten*	*warteten*

As you can see from the above table, there are no new conjugational endings to learn for the past tense.

This past tense formation is called *das Imperfekt* in German. It is used primarily to show that something was done often (*Sie spielte oft Tennis.* / She played tennis often.) or in a narrative that describes events that happen in sequence. Unlike English, German has one past tense form.

▶ **Comparing English and German Past Tense Forms**

English Past Tenses	German Past Tense
we were learning	*wir lernten*
we learned	*wir lernten*

Forming Questions in the Past Tense

It is easy to ask questions in the past tense. There is no special formula for forming past tense questions. What you already know about questions in the present tense also applies to the past tense.

In German questions the verb always comes before the subject: *Hast du einen Hund?* (Do you have a dog?). This is true even when an interrogative word begins the sentence: *Was hast du?* (What do you have?). For past tense questions, merely form the past tense stem and put the proper conjugational ending on the verb.

▶ **Contrasting Present Tense and Past Tense Questions**

Present Tense	Past Tense
Spielst du Tennis? (Do you play tennis?)	*Spieltest du Tennis?* (Did you play tennis?)
Brauchen Sie Geld? (Do you need money?)	*Brauchten Sie Geld?* (Did you need money?)

Present Tense	Past Tense
Hören Sie Radio? (Do you listen to the radio?)	*Hörten Sie Radio?* (Did you listen to the radio?)
Lernst du Deutsch? (Are you learning German?)	*Lerntest du Deutsch?* (Did you learn German?)
Wo wohnt er? (Where does he live?)	*Wo wohnte er?* (Where did he live?)
Wer arbeitet hier? (Who works here?)	*Wer arbeitete hier?* (Who worked here?)
Wen besucht er? (Whom is he visiting?)	*Wen besuchte er?* (Whom did he visit?)
Was kauft ihr? (What are you all buying?)	*Was kauftet ihr?* (What did you all buy?)

The Past Tense of Irregular Verbs

The German past tense has a long list of verbs that change to the past tense by irregular stem formations. That sounds like trouble, but for English speakers it's really not so bad. These verbs are often called "strong verbs." In this book they're just going to be called "irregular."

What you already know about the past tense will help you to use irregular verbs in the past. Regular verbs simply put a *–te* on the end of the stem of the verb. Then the conjugational ending is added.

But irregular verbs do something different, and it's exactly what irregular verbs do in English: They form a completely new stem. Let's look at some examples in English.

▶ **Verb Stems of the English Irregular Past Tense**

Infinitive	Past Tense Stem	Infinitive	Past Tense Stem
to come	came	to bring	brought

| to see | saw | to drive | drove |
| to run | ran | to go | went |

If you think about it, you can come up with a very long list of irregular verbs in English. You know them because you slowly absorbed them during your childhood.

Comparing English and German in the Past Tense

As American kids grow up, they make mistakes: Little Johnny might say, "I drinked all my milk, Mom." But he's only five years old. In time, he'll know that the past tense of "drink" is "drank."

German kids do the same thing. For a while they form all their past tense verbs like regular verbs with a *–te* ending. But eventually they begin to remember the irregularities and use the past tense of these verbs correctly.

And you will do the same thing. You'll discover that German irregular past tense forms follow very closely the pattern of English past tense forms.

Let's look at a list of some frequently used verbs so you can see what happens in both languages.

▶ **Irregular Verbs in English and German**

English Infinitive	Past Tense Stem	German Infinitive	Past Tense Stem
to break	broke	brechen	brach
to bring	brought	bringen	brachte
to come	came	kommen	kam
to drink	drank	trinken	trank
to fly	flew	fliegen	flog
to go	went	gehen	ging
to see	saw	sehen	sah
to sing	sang	singen	sang

English Infinitive	Past Tense Stem	German Infinitive	Past Tense Stem
to speak	spoke	*sprechen*	*sprach*
to stand	stood	*stehen*	*stand*

Remember that the simple past tense (*das Imperfekt*) is used in narratives and to show repetition.

What are some of the verbs that require stem changes in the past tense? The following table is a list of some common verbs that are irregular in the past tense. Notice how many follow a pattern similar to the English past tense.

▶ Irregular Past Tense Stems

English Infinitive	German Infinitive	Past Tense Stem
to bake	*backen*	*buk* (or *backte*)
to be called	*heißen*	*hieß*
to become	*werden*	*wurde*
to drive	*fahren*	*fuhr*
to eat	*essen*	*aß*
to find	*finden*	*fand*
to give	*geben*	*gab*
to have	*haben*	*hatte*
to help	*helfen*	*half*
to hit	*schlagen*	*schlug*
to know	*wissen*	*wusste*
to know, be acquainted	*kennen*	*kannte*
to let	*lassen*	*ließ*
to meet	*treffen*	*traf*
to read	*lesen*	*las*
to run	*laufen*	*lief*
to sleep	*schlafen*	*schlief*
to take	*nehmen*	*nahm*

English Infinitive	German Infinitive	Past Tense Stem
to think	denken	dachte
to wash	waschen	wusch
to wear, carry	tragen	trug
to write	schreiben	schrieb

Conjugations in the German Irregular Past Tense

You recall from previous chapters that German verbs always have to have conjugational endings. That's also true in the irregular past tense. You already know those endings.

▶ Irregular Past Tense Conjugations

Pronoun	kommen	gehen	sehen
ich	kam	ging	sah
du	kamst	gingst	sahst
er/sie/es	kam	ging	sah
wir	kamen	gingen	sahen
ihr	kamt	gingt	saht
Sie	kamen	gingen	sahen
sie (pl.)	kamen	gingen	sahen

As you can see, there's nothing new about the conjugation of the irregular past tense. Once you know the stem, you merely use the endings you already know.

Did you notice that, like in the past tense of regular verbs, the pronouns *ich, er, sie,* and *es* do not add a conjugational ending to the stem?

The Importance of Being

The infinitive *sein* is a very important verb. It's used as frequently in German as "to be" is used in English. You are very familiar with it in the present tense. But now it's time to become familiar with its past tense.

Just like English "to be," German *sein* makes a complete transformation in the past tense. "To be" becomes "was." *Sein* becomes *war.* You'll find that, like other irregular verbs, conjugating *war* is a snap.

▶ **The Past Tense of *sein***

Person	English	German
First (sing.)	I was	*ich war*
Second (sing.)	you were	*du warst*
Third (sing.)	he/she/it was	*er/sie/es war*
First (pl.)	we were	*wir waren*
Second (pl.)	you all were	*ihr wart*
Second (formal)	you were	*Sie waren*
Third (pl.)	they were	*sie waren*

A Special Look at Haben *and* Werden

These are two very common verbs in German. Alone they mean "to have" and "to become," respectively. But they have another use—these verbs, along with *sein,* will be used to form the more complex perfect tenses. Watch out for these two! *Haben* and *werden* are irregular in both the present and past tenses.

▶ **The Past Tense of *haben***

Person	Conjugation
First (sing.)	*ich hatte*
Second (sing.)	*du hattest*
Third (sing.)	*er/sie/es hatte*
First (pl.)	*wir hatten*
Second (pl.)	*ihr hattet*
Second (formal)	*Sie hatten*
Third (pl.)	*sie hatten*

▶ The Past Tense of *werden*

Person	Conjugation
First (sing.)	*ich wurde*
Second (sing.)	*du wurdest*
Third (sing.)	*er/sie/es wurde*
First (pl.)	*wir wurden*
Second (pl.)	*ihr wurdet*
Second (formal)	*Sie wurden*
Third (pl.)	*sie wurden*

Future Tense

Knowing the past tense is great for talking about things that have already happened. But what about the plans you're making for next summer or even next weekend? In this section you'll learn how to use the future tense. You'll also learn how to use the imperative form of verbs to give commands. Ready? Go!

The future tense is so simple to use. You just use a present tense conjugation in the context of a future tense meaning.

- *Heute geht Karl in die Schule.* (Karl's going to school today.)
- *Morgen geht Karl in die Schule.* (Karl's going to school tomorrow.)

But just as English has a more specific way of forming the future tense, so does German. Its formation is very much like English. In English you simply use the verb "shall" or "will" and follow it with the verb that describes what will be done in the future:

- ■ I go there.   I shall go there.
- ■ You are late.   You will be late.
- ■ Mother has a problem.   Mother will have a problem.*

Using

The other way to form the future tense is really quite simple. It has to do with another use of a verb you already know: *werden*. To form the future tense, conjugate *werden* and follow it by the infinitive that describes what will be done in the future. But be careful! In German the infinitive has to be the last word in the sentence—no matter how long the sentence might get. How about some examples?

- ■ *Er wird nach Hause gehen.* (He will go home.)
- ■ *Die Kinder werden morgen im Park spielen.* (Tomorrow the children will play in the park.)
- ■ *Ich werde am Sonnabend in die Stadt fahren.* (I will drive to the city on Saturday.)

*Did you notice that English has two tense forms for each tense? For each of those pairs, German always has only one tense.

Present, Past, and Future

You have already become acquainted with three important tenses in German. With these three you can speak about anything that has happened, that is happening, or that will happen.

There are three "signal" words that tell you what tense to use: *heute* (today), *gestern* (yesterday), and *morgen* (tomorrow). *Heute* is the signal for the present tense, *gestern* for the past tense, and *morgen* for the future tense.

Let's look at how the three tenses differ in form and meaning with regular verbs.

▶ **Contrasting the Present, Past, and Future Tenses**

Tense	English	German
Present	I am learning German.	*Ich lerne Deutsch.*
Present	I learn German.	*Ich lerne Deutsch.*
Past	I was learning German.	*Ich lernte Deutsch.*
Past	I learned German.	*Ich lernte Deutsch.*
Future	I will be learning German.	*Ich werde Deutsch lernen.*
Future	I will learn German.	*Ich werde Deutsch lernen.*

Look at the sentences below and notice how the three tenses differ in verb formation and usage.

> **Present** *Heute bin ich in der Hauptstadt.* (I am in the capital city today.)
> **Past** *Gestern war ich in der Hauptstadt.* (I was in the capital city yesterday.)
> **Future** *Morgen werde ich in der Hauptstadt sein.* (I will be in the capital city tomorrow.)

Future Tense with Irregular Verbs

Because in the future tense you use *werden* plus an infinitive, the irregular verbs are very easy to use in the future tense. There's no stem change to remember. Remember that when you form the future tense of any verb, you conjugate *werden* and place the conjugated verb "as an infinitive" at the end of the sentence. That means that you have to change any irregularity in the present tense back to the verb's infinitive form, when restating a sentence in the future tense.

▶ **Contrasting the Present and Future Tenses of Irregular Verbs**

Present Tense	Future Tense
Er liest die Zeitung. (He reads the newspaper.)	*Er wird die Zeitung lesen.* (He will read the newspaper.)
Sie läuft in die Schule. (She runs to school.)	*Sie wird in die Schule laufen.* (She will run to school.)
Sabine trägt einen neuen Hut. (Sabine is wearing a new hat.)	*Sabine wird einen neuen Hut tragen.* (Sabine will wear a new hat.)
Das Kind spricht kein Deutsch. (The child doesn't speak any German.)	*Das Kind wird kein Deutsch sprechen.* (The child will not speak any German.)
Andreas fängt den Ball. (Andreas catches the ball.)	*Andreas wird den Ball fangen.* (Andreas will catch the ball.)
Wo trifft sie die Touristen? (Where is she meeting the tourists?)	*Wo wird sie die Touristen treffen?* (Where will she meet the tourists?)

Prefixes

You probably have noticed by now that many German words appear with different prefixes. Those prefixes change the meaning of a word, but they don't change how the basic word functions. For example, an irregular verb is still irregular no matter what the prefix might be.

Prefixes aren't unique to German. There are many in English, and they alter the meaning of words just like German prefixes. In the following table, notice how the meaning of a word is changed by adding a prefix.

▶ Prefixes with German Words

Prefix	Basic Word	Meaning	Prefix Added	New Meaning
be–	*kommen*	to come	*bekommen*	to receive
an–	*kommen*	to come	*ankommen*	to arrive
er–	*schlagen*	to hit	*erschlagen*	to kill, strike dead
auf–	*schlagen*	to hit	*aufschlagen*	to open (a book)
bei–	*bringen*	to bring	*beibringen*	to teach
um–	*bringen*	to bring	*umbringen*	to murder

Inseparable Prefixes

The inseparable prefixes are: *be–, ent–, emp–, er–, ge–, ver–,* and *zer–.* Here are some verbs that have these prefixes: *bekommen* (to receive, get), *entlassen* (to set free, dismiss), *empfinden* (to perceive), *erwarten* (to expect), *gehören* (to belong to), *verstehen* (to understand), and *zerbrechen* (to break to pieces).

When these prefixes are attached to a word, the accent is always on the second syllable: *besuchen* (beh-ZOOCH-en) (to visit), *gebrauchen* (geh-BROWCH-EN) (to use), *verlachen* (fair-LUCH-en) (to laugh at).

▶ Conjugating Verbs with and Without Inseparable Prefixes

Verb with No Prefix	English Meaning	Verb with Inseparable Prefix	English Meaning
ich komme	I come	*ich bekomme*	I receive
er wartet	he waits	*er erwartet*	he expects
wir stehen	we stand	*wir verstehen*	we understand

Separable Prefixes

Some of the primary separable prefixes are: *an, auf, aus, bei, ein, her, hin, mit, nach, um,* and *weg.* To conjugate a verb with a separable prefix, place the prefix at the end of the sentence and conjugate the verb normally. For example, the infinitive: *ansehen* (to look at) in the present tense:

▶ Conjugating a Verb with a Separable Prefix

Ich sehe . . . an.
Du siehst . . . an.
Er sieht . . . an.
Wir sehen . . . an.
Ihr seht . . . an.
Sie sehen . . . an.

Add the following words to your vocabulary and take careful note of how the prefixes change the meaning of the words.

- *hören* (to hear)
- *aufhören* (to stop, cease)
- *nehmen* (to take)
- *stehen* (to stand)
- *verstehen* (to understand)

Be savvy about prefixes. Always check out the prefix of a word before assuming what the word means. Although you know that *stehen* means "to stand," that information can't necessarily help you to know what *entstehen* means. (By the way, *entstehen* means "to originate.") You know that *nehmen* means "to take." But the meaning of the verb *er nimmt . . . an* and of the verb *er nimmt . . . ab* has been altered to "he assumes" and "he reduces." Never underestimate the importance of the prefix.

Using German well means knowing prefixes and using them properly.

Direct Objects

To discover the direct object in a sentence, just ask "what" or "whom" with the verb. Examples:

▶ **Finding the Direct Object**

Sentence	What or Whom?	Direct Object
John buys a car.	What does John buy?	car
I like it.	What do I like?	it
She sent a long list of problems	What did she send?	list

German is very similar to English in that some nouns—feminine and neuter nouns, specifically—don't make any changes when they're used as direct objects. And just like English, most German pronouns do require changes. Look at these examples:

▶ **German Nouns and Pronouns as Direct Objects**

Noun as Subject	Noun as Direct Object
Die Schule ist in der Stadt. (The school is in the city.)	*Sie* (pl.) *sehen die Schule.* (They see the school.)
Die Lehrerin ist da. (The teacher is there.)	*Sie* (pl.) *sehen die Lehrerin.* (They see the teacher.)

Pronoun as Subject	Pronoun as Direct Object
Ich bin in Berlin. (I am in Berlin.)	*Sie* (pl.) *sehen mich.* (They see me.)
Du bist in Hamburg. (You are in Hamburg.)	*Sie* (pl.) *sehen dich.* (They see you.)

Nominative and Accusative

The nominative case is the name given to the subject of a sentence. The subject is said to be in the nominative case.

■ English: The boy is going to the park.
■ German: *Der Junge geht zum Park.*

Direct objects are said to be in the accusative case.

■ English: My brother knows the teacher.
■ German: *Mein Bruder kennt den Lehrer.*

Whenever you change a masculine noun from *der Mann* to *den Mann,* you have changed it from the nominative to the accusative case. And with feminine and neuter nouns, the nominative and accusative cases are identical. This is also true of plural nouns.

■ *Mein Bruder kennt den Lehrer.* (My brother knows the teacher.)
■ *Mein Bruder kennt die Lehrer.* (My brother knows the teachers.)

▶ **Definite and Indefinite Articles in the Accusative Case**

Masculine	Feminine	Neuter	Plural
den	die	das	die
einen	eine	ein	keine

A verb that is often followed by a direct object is *haben* (to have). Look at these examples:

- *Sie* (pl.) *haben die Zeitung.*
  (They have the newspaper.)
- *Wir haben ein Problem.* (We have a problem.)

▶ Pronouns in the Accusative Case

Person	Nominative Pronoun	Accusative Pronoun	English Meaning
First (sing.)	*ich*	*mich*	me
Second (sing.)	*du*	*dich*	you
Third (sing.)	*er/sie/es*	*ihn/sie/es*	him/her/it
First (pl.)	*wir*	*uns*	us
Second (pl.)	*ihr*	*euch*	you
Second (formal)	*Sie*	*Sie*	you
Third (pl.)	*sie*	*sie*	them

Using Adjectives with Direct Objects

You learned that masculine nouns as direct objects change to the accusative case. That means that *der Mann* becomes *den Mann*. The same *–en* ending occurs when an adjective is added: *der alte Mann* becomes *den alten Mann* in the accusative case. Since the feminine, neuter, and plural are identical in both the nominative and accusative cases, there is no change in the adjective ending when they are used as direct objects.

Look at the pattern of adjective endings in the nominative and accusative cases.

▶ Comparing the Nominative and Accusative Cases

Case	Masculine	Feminine	Neuter	Plural
Nom.	*der kleine Tisch*	*die kleine Flasche*	*das kleine Buch*	*die kleinen Bücher*
Acc.	*den kleinen Tisch*	*die kleine Flasche*	*das kleine Buch*	*die kleinen Bücher*

Let's look at some examples using adjectives with direct objects:

- *Der neue Schüler wohnt in Deutschland.* (The new student lives in Germany.)
- *Wir besuchen den neuen Schüler.* (We visit the new student.)
- *Die arme Frau kommt aus Österreich.* (The poor woman comes from Austria.)
- *Hören Sie die arme Frau?* (Do you hear the poor woman?)

Prepositions That Take the Accusative

The accusative case is also required after certain prepositions

- *bis* (to, till)
- *ohne* (without)
- *durch* (through)
- *um* (around, at)
- *für* (for)
- *wider* (against)
- *gegen* (against)

▶ Accusative Case with Direct Objects and Prepositions

Gender	Direct Object	Preposition
Masculine	*Ich sehe den Mann.* (I see the man.)	*Es ist für den Mann.* (It is for the man.)
Feminine	*Ich sehe die Frau.* (I see the woman.)	*Es ist für die Frau.* (It is for the woman.)
Neuter	*Ich sehe das Kind.* (I see the child.)	*Es ist für das Kind.* (It is for the child.)

Gender	Direct Object	Preposition
Plural	*Ich sehe die Kinder.* (I see the children.)	*Es ist für die Kinder.* (It is for the children.)

It works the same way with pronouns.

▶ Accusative Pronouns with Prepositions

Pronoun	Direct Object	Preposition
ich	*Sie sehen mich.* (They see me.)	*Es ist für mich.* (It's for me.)
du	*Sie sehen dich.* (They see you.)	*Es ist für dich.* (It's for you.)
er	*Sie sehen ihn.* (They see him.)	*Es ist für ihn.* (It's for him.)
sie (sing.)	*Sie sehen sie.* (They see her.)	*Es ist für sie.* (It's for her.)
wir	*Sie sehen uns.* (They see us.)	*Es ist für uns.* (It's for us.)
ihr	*Sie sehen euch.* (They see you all.)	*Es ist für euch.* (It's for you all.)
Sie (formal)	*Sie sehen Sie.* (They see you.)	*Es ist für Sie.* (It's for you.)
sie (pl.)	*Sie sehen sie.* (They see them.)	*Es ist für sie.* (It's for them.)

Indirect Objects

It may sound like just another confusing grammatical term, but an indirect object is something that you are already very familiar with. You use it every day in English. It's really quite simple to identify in a sentence. Ask "for whom" or "to whom" something is being done and the answer is the indirect object. See the following for some examples in English:

▶ Identifying Indirect Objects

The Sentence		The Indirect Object
Ask "for whom" or	"to whom"	
He gave her a dollar.	To whom did he give a dollar?	her

The Sentence Ask "for whom" or	"to whom"	The Indirect Object
We sent them a letter.	To whom did we send a letter?	them
I bought you a ring.	For whom did I buy a ring?	you

In German the indirect object is indicated by the dative case. Like the accusative case, this case requires changes to the definite and indefinite articles of nouns.

▶ Definite Articles in the Dative Case

Masculine	Feminine	Neuter	Plural
dem	der	dem	den

You'll see that, unlike with the accusative case, which changed only masculine nouns, all nouns and pronouns make a slight change when used in the dative case. Masculine and neuter words change *der* and *das* to *dem*. Feminine nouns change *die* to *der.* And plural nouns change the article *die* to *den.*

Indefinite articles also take different endings when they are used in the dative case.

▶ Indefinite Articles in the Dative Case

Masculine	Feminine	Neuter	Plural
einem	einer	einem	keinen

In addition to these changes to the definite and indefinite articles, plural nouns also require an ending on the noun itself. In the dative plural the noun must end with an extra *–n* if there isn't already one in the plural nominative: *mit zwei Heften.* Take a close look at the following examples to see how the dative endings are used in comparison with the nominative and accusative cases.

▶ The Nominative, Accusative, and Dative Cases of Nouns

Gender	Nominative	Accusative	Dative
Masculine	der Mann	den Mann	dem Mann
Masculine	ein Mann	einen Mann	einem Mann
Feminine	die Lampe	die Lampe	der Lampe
Feminine	eine Lampe	eine Lampe	einer Lampe
Neuter	das Heft	das Heft	dem Heft
Neuter	ein Heft	ein Heft	einem Heft
Plural	die Hefte	die Hefte	den Heften
Plural	keine Hefte	keine Hefte	keinen Heften

Let's look at some sentences that demonstrate the use of the dative with an indirect object:

- *Die Männer geben der alten Frau ein Brötchen.* (The men give the old lady a bread roll.)
- *Der Vater kaufte seinem Sohn ein Fahrrad.* (The father bought his son a bicycle.)

Changing Dative Nouns to Pronouns

You have already learned how to change nominative and accusative nouns to pronouns. The same idea is used when changing dative nouns to pronouns.

The key to making the change correctly is identifying the gender of the noun. If the noun is masculine or neuter, change to the pronoun *ihm*. If the noun is feminine, change to the pronoun *ihr*. And if the noun is plural, change to the pronoun *ihnen*. You already know that a noun combined with *ich* (*mein Vater und ich*) is replaced by *wir*. Therefore, if the noun/*ich* phrase is in the dative case, change it to the pronoun *uns*. Let's look at some examples.

▶ Pronouns in the Dative Case

Person	Nominative	Dative	English
First (sing.)	*ich*	*mir*	me
Second (sing.)	*du*	*dir*	you
Third (sing.)	*er*	*ihm*	him
Third (sing.)	*sie*	*ihr*	her
Third (sing.)	*es*	*ihm*	it
First (pl.)	*wir*	*uns*	us
Second (pl.)	*ihr*	*euch*	you all
Second (formal)	*Sie*	*Ihnen*	you
Third (pl.)	*sie*	*ihnen*	them

Notice that the dative forms of *Sie* and *sie* (pl.) are identical except for the capitalization of *Sie* and *Ihnen*.

Some example sentences with dative pronouns as indirect objects:

■ *Er gibt ihm ein Geschenk.* (He gives him a gift.) (To whom? Him.)
■ *Wir kaufen ihr einen Hut.* (We buy her a hat.) (For whom? Her.)

Dative nouns and pronouns also follow the dative prepositions: *aus, außer, bei, gegenüber, mit, nach, seit, von,* and *zu* (out, apart from, at, opposite, with, after, since, from, to).

▶ Replacing Dative Nouns with Pronouns

Noun in the Dative Case	Pronoun Replacement for the Dative Noun
Ich gebe dem Kind einen Bleistift.	*Ich gebe ihm einen Bleistift.* (I give him a pencil.)
Sie tanzt mit meinem Vater.	*Sie tanzt mit ihm.* (She is dancing with him.)
Mark wohnt bei seiner Tante.	*Mark wohnt bei ihr.* (Mark lives with her.)
Er kaufte den Kindern Schokolade.	*Er kaufte ihnen Schokolade.* (He bought them chocolate.)
Sie bekommt einen Brief von Hans und mir.	*Sie bekommt einen Brief von uns.* (She receives a letter from us.)

Sentences Can Be Chock Full of Pronouns!

Have you noticed that sentences that contain an indirect object also have a direct object in them? *Sie gibt ihrem Vater das Buch.* (She gives her father the book.) To whom does she give the book? *Ihrem Vater* is the indirect object. What does she give to her father? *Das Buch* is the direct object.

You've practiced changing either the indirect object noun or the direct object noun to a pronoun. But it's possible to change both to pronouns. You do it in English, but you may add a word when you do so. You place the preposition "to" or "for" in front of the pronoun that has replaced the indirect object. Look at these examples of changing both the direct object and indirect object nouns to pronouns:

■   Mary sent the man some sandwiches.
    Mary sent them **to** him.
■   We bought Sally a new toy.
    We bought it **for** her.

German doesn't have to add a preposition when changing indirect and direct object nouns to pronouns. But there is a little switch made: The indirect object pronoun changes position with the direct object pronoun. Take a look at some examples:

■   *Ich gebe dem Mann eine Tasse. Ich gebe sie ihm.*
■   *Erich kaufte seiner Schwester ein Fahrrad.*
    Erich kaufte es ihr.

Dative case nouns and pronouns are also used after the dative prepositions: *aus, außer, bei, gegenüber, mit, nach, seit, von,* and *zu* (out, apart from, at, opposite, with, after, since, from, to). For example: *mit dem Mann* (with the man), *von ihr* (from her).

04 / Putting It All Together

Questions

You've already seen a few questions in German through-out the first few chapters of this book. In this chapter you'll have a detailed look at questions and the interrogative words used to ask them.

The Three Types of Questions

There are three ways of asking a question:

- Intone a statement like a question. *Thomas ist krank?* (Thomas is sick?)
- Reverse the position of the subject and the verb. *Ist Thomas krank?* (Is Thomas sick?)
- Begin the sentence with an interrogative word. *Warum ist Thomas krank?* (Why is Thomas sick?)

Placing a Verb First

When a sentence is changed to a question, the only change in German is the position of the verb and the sub-ject. It doesn't matter if the subject is a noun or a pronoun.

Invert the order of the two so that the verb comes first in the question:

- *Wir sind hier.* (We are here.)
- *Sind wir hier?* (Are we here?)
- *Karl hat ein Buch.* (Karl has a book.)
- *Hat Karl ein Buch?* (Does Karl have a book?)
  Compare the German and English:

▶ Questions in the Negative

English Question	German Question
Isn't he sick?	Ist er nicht krank?
Aren't you in school?	Bist du nicht in der Schule?
Don't I know him?	Kenne ich ihn nicht?
Doesn't she have a book?	Hat sie kein Buch?

With nearly all English verbs, questions are formed by beginning the question with "do" or "does." This never happens in German. "To be" is one of the few English verbs that doesn't require "do" or "does" to form a question: Is she at home? Are you alone?

Interrogative Words

Another way to form a question is to use an interrogative (or "question word"). There are several interrogative words, and each one asks something different. Look at the following table for some examples.

- *Ist Hans da?* (Is Hans there?)
- *Sind Sie Amerikanerin?* (Are you an American?)
- *Wie heißen Sie?* (What is your name? Literally: "How are you called?")
- *Wer ist das?* (Who is that?)

▶ Interrogative Words

The Kind of Question	Interrogative	The Question	A Possible Answer
where someone is	wo?	Wo ist dein Vater? (Where is your father?)	Er ist zu Hause. (He is at home.)
where someone is going	wohin?	Wohin geht Hans? (Where is Hans going?)	Er geht ins Kino. (He is going to the movies.)
where someone is coming from	woher?	Woher kommst du? (Where are you coming from?)	Ich komme aus Amerika. (I come from America.)
who someone is	wer?	Wer ist er? (Who is he?)	Er ist der Lehrer. (He is the teacher.)
how someone does something	wie?	Wie spielt er Tennis? (How does he play tennis?)	Er spielt gut Tennis. (He plays tennis well.)
when something is done	wann?	Wann kommst du nach Hause? (When are you coming home?)	Ich komme um elf Uhr nach Hause. (I'm coming home at eleven o'clock.)
what something is	was?	Was hast du? (What do you have?)	Ich habe einen neuen Hut. (I have a new hat.)
what kind of	was für?	Was für ein Buch ist das? (What kind of book is that?)	Das ist ein Lehrbuch. (That is a textbook.)
why something is done	warum?	Warum ist er müde? (Why is he tired?)	Er ist sehr alt. (He is very old.)

Asking Where

The German language has three specific forms of the question "where": *wo, wohin,* and *woher.* The three forms are really three different concepts about location. *Wo* always asks at what location a person is. *Wohin* asks to what location a person is going. And *woher* wants to know from what location someone comes.

Wo asks "where" a person is: *Wo bist du jetzt?* (Where are you now?) By using the preposition *in,* you can give a large variety of answers to the question "where" when you use city and country names. Many are the same in both English and German: *in Berlin, in Bonn, in New York, in Amerika, in Deutschland.*

■ *Wo ist Liese?* (Where is Liese?) *Sie ist in London.* (She is in London.)

■ *Wo bist du?* (Where are you?) *Du bist in Berlin.* (You are in Berlin.)

The question word *wohin* is used to ask where someone is going with verbs of motion: *Wohin gehst du?* (Where are you going?) *Wohin fliegen Sie?* (Where are you flying?) *Wohin fährst du?* (Where are you driving?)

If the place you're going is the item in a sentence that you want to question, you have to ask "where to?" Use *wohin* in this case.

■ *Wohin fährt der Kellner?* (Where's the waiter driving?) *Der Kellner fährt nach Schweden.* (The waiter is driving to Sweden.)

What if you're asking where someone came from? That's where the third question word for "where" comes in. *Woher* asks "from where?" *Woher kommst du?* (Where do you come from?)

Asking How and When

Adverbs—whether in German or English—tell you something about the verb: how, where, or when something is done.

You have already used several adverbial phrases: *Es geht Andreas gut.* (Andreas is doing well.) *Heute gehe ich nach Hause.* (Today I am going home.) *Im Winter ist es kalt.* (In winter it is cold.) Here are a few more practical adverbs to add to your vocabulary:

- *langsam* (slowly)
- *laut* (loudly)
- *leise* (quietly)
- *schnell* (fast)

Let's look at some sample questions and answers using *wie.*

- *Wie fährt dein Bruder?* (How does your brother drive?)
- *Er fährt sehr schnell.* (He drives very fast.)
- *Wie sprechen wir?* (How do we speak?)
- *Wir sprechen langsam.* (We speak slowly.)

Asking Who

To ask who someone is, use the interrogative *wer. Wer ist das?* means "Who is that?"

- *Wer ist der Mann?* (Who is the man?)
- *Der Mann ist Herr Schmidt.* (The man is Mr. Smith.)

- *Wer ist das Mädchen?* (Who is the little girl?)
- *Das Mädchen ist Petra.* (The little girl is Petra.)

Asking Why

Was für asks about the characteristics of someone or something: color, size, quality. *Was für ein Mädchen ist sie?* (What kind of a girl is she?) *Sie ist ein sehr nettes Mädchen.* (She's a very nice girl.) Don't confuse *was für* with *was,* which asks only "what."

The word for why is *warum.* This asks for a reason. The English response to why (*warum?*) something is done, is given with the conjunction "because": "Why did he leave her?" "He left her because they fell out of love." The German word for "because" is *denn. Warum geht er nach Hause?* (Why does he go home?) *Er geht nach Hause, denn er ist müde.* (He goes home because he's tired.) Use *denn* to show the reason for some action.

Commands

Kaiser Wilhelm hasn't been around since 1918, but giving commands in German still takes place without him. The imperative, as it's called, is quite simple in German.

In English, you can take any infinitive (to run, to hide, to spell), drop the word "to," and you have an imperative form: *run to the store.* German is a bit different but just as easy.

We'll start with the formal command form. Begin with an infinitive: *gehen.* Place the pronoun *Sie* (formal you) behind it, and you have the German imperative: *Gehen Sie!* (Go!) Note that the German imperative requires an exclamation point after it.

Only one verb requires a little spelling change to form the imperative: *sein*. An *–e* is added after the letter *i*. Then follow the word with *Sie* and you have: *Seien Sie!* (Be!)

Here are a few examples:

- ■ *Bleiben Sie da!* (Stay there.)
- ■ *Fahren Sie schneller!* (Drive faster.)
- ■ *Essen Sie!* (Eat.)
- ■ *Fliegen Sie nach Berlin!* (Fly to Berlin.)

Informal Commands

In addition to the *Sie* (formal) version of commands, there are ways to give commands to those whom you know on a less formal basis, using the two other words for "you" in German: *du* and its plural, *ihr*. You cannot use the formal command with people to whom you say *du*. There are informal imperative formations, and they are really quite simple.

For informal singular (*du*), take the stem of the verb and add *–e*:

- ■ *Gehe!* (Go.)
- ■ *Bleibe!* (Stay.)
- ■ *Komme!* (Come.)

If the verb is irregular in the present tense by a vowel change (*–e* to *–i* or *–ie*), make that change in the verb stem, but do not add an *–e* on the end:

- ■ *Gib!* (Give.)
- ■ *Sprich!* (Speak.)
- ■ *Sei!* (Be.)

For the informal plural (*ihr*), just use the regular present tense conjugation. It's also the imperative of the verb:

- *Geht!* (Go.)
- *Bleibt!* (Stay.)
- *Seid!* (Be.)

Express Yourself with Feeling Verbs

In both English and German there are certain words that put "emotion" or "a special spin" on a sentence. They're often called auxiliaries or helping words.

There are six modal auxiliaries in German. Below they are shown conjugated in the present tense. Their infinitives and meaning are: *dürfen* (may), *können* (can, to be able to), *mögen* (to like), *müssen* (must, to have to), *sollen* (should, ought to), and *wollen* (to want). Notice the irregularity with *ich, du, er, sie, es.*

▶ Present Tense of *dürfen* (may, to be allowed to)

Singular Person	Conjugation	Plural Person	Conjugation
First (sing.)	ich darf	First (pl.)	wir dürfen
Second (sing.)	du darfst	Second (pl.)	ihr dürft
		Second (formal)	Sie dürfen
Third (sing.)	er/sie/es darf	Third (pl.)	sie dürfen

▶ Present Tense of *können* (can, to be able to)

Singular Person	Conjugation	Plural Person	Conjugation
First (sing.)	ich kann	First (pl.)	wir können
Second (sing.)	du kannst	Second (pl.)	ihr könnt
		Second (formal)	Sie können
Third (sing.)	er/sie/es kann	Third (pl.)	sie können

▶ **Present Tense of *mögen* (to like)**

Singular Person	Conjugation	Plural Person	Conjugation
First (sing.)	*ich mag*	First (pl.)	*wir mögen*
Second (sing.)	*du magst*	Second (pl.)	*ihr mögt*
		Second (formal)	*Sie mögen*
Third (sing.)	*er/sie/es mag*	Third (pl.)	*sie mögen*

▶ **Present Tense of *müssen* (must, to have to)**

Singular Person	Conjugation	Plural Person	Conjugation
First (sing.)	*ich muss*	First (pl.)	*wir müssen*
Second (sing.)	*du musst*	Second (pl.)	*ihr müsst*
		Second (formal)	*Sie müssen*
Third (sing.)	*er/sie/es muss*	Third (pl.)	*sie müssen*

▶ **Present Tense of *sollen* (should, ought to)**

Singular Person	Conjugation	Plural Person	Conjugation
First (sing.)	*ich soll*	First (pl.)	*wir sollen*
Second (sing.)	*du sollst*	Second (pl.)	*ihr sollt*
		Second (formal)	*Sie sollen*
Third (sing.)	*er/sie/es soll*	Third (pl.)	*sie sollen*

▶ **Present Tense of *wollen* (to want)**

Singular Person	Conjugation	Plural Person	Conjugation
First (sing.)	*ich will*	First (pl.)	*wir wollen*
Second (sing.)	*du willst*	Second (pl.)	*ihr wollt*
		Second (formal)	*Sie wollen*
Third (sing.)	*er/sie/es will*	Third (pl.)	*sie wollen*

Notice how the meaning of a sentence is altered by the addition of a modal auxiliary.

■ *Er besucht seinen Onkel.* (He visits his uncle.)
■ *Er darf seinen Onkel besuchen.* (He may visit his uncle.)

■   *Er kann seinen Onkel besuchen.*
     (He can visit his uncle.)
■   *Er muss seinen Onkel besuchen.*
     (He has to visit his uncle.)
■   *Er soll seinen Onkel besuchen.*
     (He should visit his uncle.)
■   *Er will seinen Onkel besuchen.*
     (He wants to visit his uncle.)

One of the keys to accuracy is to remember to place the infinitive at the end of the sentence: *Er will seinen Onkel besuchen.*

Watch out for *können* and *mögen!* The modal auxiliary *können* has a special function. It's used *alone* in a sentence to infer that someone knows a language and that he or she can read, write, speak, and understand that language. For example: *Er kann Deutsch.* (He knows German. In other words, he can read, write, speak, and understand German.)

In the past tense the modal auxiliaries follow the pattern of regular verbs. But the Umlaut is omitted throughout the past tense conjugation.

Idiomatic Expressions

Did you know that German has slang and idiomatic expressions just like English? And they're just as strange sounding as English slang and idioms are when translated literally.

Imagine a person who's just learning English, hearing someone say, "Get a load of her!" What must he or she think? The same thing occurs when English speakers learn German: They hear a lot of weird expressions that don't seem to make much sense when they look the words up in a dictionary. That's because they're idioms or just plain slang, and direct translations are impossible.

Let's take a look at some interesting German phrases and their English idiomatic counterparts:

- *Das ist mir egal.* (I don't care.)
- *Das ist reiner Quatsch!* (That's a lot of baloney.)
- *Du nimmst mich auf den Arm.*
  (You're pulling my leg.)
- *Er murmelte etwas in seinen Bart.* (He mumbled something under his breath.)
- *Halt's Maul!* (Shut up! Hold your tongue!)
- *Hau ab!* (Get out! Knock it off!)
- *Ich habe mit ihm ein Hühnchen zu rupfen.* (I've got a bone to pick with him.)
- *Mensch! Das ist ja toll!* (Man! That's just great!)
- *Mir hängt der ganze Kram zum Halse heraus.* (I'm fed up with the whole thing.)
- *Schieß los!* (Get going.)
- *Seine Frau ist in andern Umständen.* (His wife's in the family way.)

Using slang and idioms in a foreign language takes courage, because you may not read circumstances correctly and might use a word or phrase at the worst possible moment or with the wrong person. You certainly wouldn't ask your mother-in-law to leave the room by saying, *"Hau ab!"* to her. Experiment, but be cautious.

What's Yours? Possessives

Just like English, German shows "to whom" something belongs by using a possessive adjective. *Mein* means "my," and *dein* means "your." The German possessive adjectives require endings that show gender—just like *ein* and *kein*. Look at these examples:

▶ Gender with Possessive Adjectives

Masculine Nouns	Feminine Nouns	Neuter Nouns	Plural Nouns
der Freund	die Schule	das Haus	die Freunde
ein Freund	eine Schule	ein Haus	zehn Freunde
kein Freund	keine Schule	kein Haus	keine Freunde
mein Freund	meine Schule	mein Haus	meine Freunde
dein Freund	deine Schule	dein Haus	deine Freunde

When masculine nouns are used as direct objects, the ending *–en* is required on the article, on *kein,* or on the possessive adjectives (*mein, dein*): *Ich sehe den Freund. Ich sehe einen Freund. Ich sehe keinen Freund. Ich sehe meinen Freund. Ich sehe deinen Freund.*

The Rest of the Possessive Adjectives

The possessive adjectives *mein* and *dein* were easy to pick up because they acted like *ein* and *kein* with nouns.

But now it's time to learn the rest of the possessive adjectives. Just as *mein* refers to the pronoun *ich,* and *dein* refers to the pronoun *du,* the remaining possessive adjectives refer to specific pronouns.

▶ Possessive Adjectives

Pronoun	Possessive Adjective	English
ich	mein	my
du	dein	your
er	sein	his
sie (sing.)	ihr	her
es	sein	its
wir	unser	our

Pronoun	Possessive Adjective	English
ihr	*euer*	your
Sie	*Ihr*	your
sie (pl.)	*ihr*	their

When you use nouns, masculine nouns will use *sein* as their possessive adjective, feminine nouns will use *ihr,* neuter nouns will use *sein,* and plural nouns will use *ihr*:

- *Der Mann findet sein Ticket.* (The man finds his ticket.)
- *Die Dame sieht ihren Sohn.* (The lady sees her son.)
- *Das Kind liebt seine Eltern.* (The child loves his parents.)
- *Die Kinder suchten ihre Bücher.* (The children looked for their books.)

Remember that the gender of the possessive adjective depends not on the noun it is modifying, but on the noun it represents. In the sentence above, "*Die Dame sieht ihren Sohn,*" the woman (*die Dame*) is feminine and therefore uses the possessive adjective *ihr* to mean "her." Her son (*der Sohn*) is masculine and the direct object, so the adjective must take the masculine ending *–en*.

Just as certain endings are required with *ein, kein, mein,* and *dein*, the same endings are required for all possessive adjectives. For example:

> **Masculine nouns**: *mein Lehrer, dein Lehrer, sein Lehrer, ihr Lehrer, unser Lehrer, euer Lehrer, Ihr Lehrer, ihr Lehrer*
> **Feminine nouns**: *meine Lampe, deine Lampe, seine Lampe, ihre Lampe, unsere Lampe, eure Lampe, Ihre Lampe, ihre Lampe*

Neuter nouns: *mein Buch, dein Buch, sein Buch, ihr Buch, unser Buch, euer Buch, Ihr Buch, ihr Buch*
Plural nouns: *meine Hefte, deine Hefte, seine Hefte, ihre Hefte, unsere Hefte, eure Hefte, Ihre Hefte, ihre Hefte*

Now let's look at the endings that are used on the possessive adjectives in the accusative case. Recall that the accusative case is used when a noun is the direct object of a sentence, or following an accusative preposition.

Masculine nouns: *meinen Lehrer, deinen Lehrer, seinen Lehrer, ihren Lehrer, unseren Lehrer, euren Lehrer, Ihren Lehrer, ihren Lehrer*
Feminine nouns: *meine Lampe, deine Lampe, seine Lampe, ihre Lampe, unsere Lampe, eure Lampe, Ihre Lampe, ihre Lampe*
Neuter nouns: *mein Buch, dein Buch, sein Buch, ihr Buch, unser Buch, euer Buch, Ihr Buch, ihr Buch*
Plural nouns: *meine Hefte, deine Hefte, seine Hefte, ihre Hefte, unsere Hefte, eure Hefte, Ihre Hefte, ihre Hefte*

If you compare these two lists, you will see that the endings in both cases are the same for feminine, neuter, and plural nouns. It is only the masculine case that takes different endings in the accusative case.

A New Case: Genitive
You're about to meet the fourth and last case in the German language. It's called the genitive and has a couple of simple and clear-cut functions. The primary use of the

genitive case is to show possession. This is done in English by apostrophe "s" (–'s) or by the preposition "of":

■ John's mother is a doctor.
■ The roar of the lion sent shivers down his spine.

German has the form that uses an –s to show possession, but you don't need an apostrophe. It's used primarily with names or descriptions of people that don't require an article:

■ *Herberts Vater* (Herbert's father)
■ *Mutters Bruder* (Mother's brother)

But the most common form used to show possession involves the use of the genitive case. An article with genitive endings is used to indicate possession.

▶ Genitive Articles

Masculine	Feminine	Neuter	Plural
des	der	des	der
eines	einer	eines	keiner

Masculine and neuter nouns require an –s ending to be added to the noun as well in the genitive case. If the noun has only one syllable, the ending is –es (*des Mannes*). If the noun has more than one syllable, the ending is –s (*des Lehrers*).

Adjectives that describe a noun in the genitive also take an ending, but it's easy to remember because it is always –en.

▶ Genitive Endings

Masculine	Feminine	Neuter	Plural
des netten Mannes	der netten Frau	des netten Kindes	der netten Kinder
eines netten Mannes	einer netten Frau	eines netten Kindes	keiner netten Kinder
Ihres netten Mannes	Ihrer netten Frau	Ihres netten Kindes	Ihrer netten Kinder

These phrases mean: "the nice man's," "the nice woman's," "the nice child's," "the nice children's," or "of the nice man," "of the nice woman," "of the nice child," "of the nice children."

The same genitive endings are used with nouns that follow genitive prepositions, such as: *anstatt, trotz, wegen,* and *während* (instead of, despite, because of, during). For example:

Trotz seiner Krankheit ging er ins Theater. (Despite his illness he went to the theater.)

Describing Things and People

Adjectives modify and describe nouns, and you've encountered quite a few of them in German already. In German, adjectives reflect the gender, case, and number of the noun they modify. In this section you'll learn more about using adjectives with the proper endings.

Antonyms and Other Words of Contrast

Pairs of words that show a contrast are helpful when giving an opinion about something. Is it good or is it bad, in your opinion? Was the play boring or interesting? Did you eat too much or too little roast beef?

The following pairs of words are antonyms or they show a strong contrast.

▶ Words of Contrast

English Pair	*German Pair*
beautiful/ugly	*hübsch/hässlich*
big/little	*groß/klein*
black/white	*schwarz/weiß*
boring/interesting	*langweilig/interessant*
cold/hot	*kalt/heiß*
dark/bright	*dunkel/hell*
dry/wet	*trocken/naß*
fashionable/old-fashioned	*modisch/altmodisch*
fast/slow	*schnell/langsam*
find/lose	*finden/verlieren*
funny/sad	*lustig/traurig*
here/there	*hier/da* (or *dort*)
high/low	*hoch/niedrig*
hungry/full	*hungrig/satt*
lazy/diligent	*faul/fleißig*
long/short	*lang/kurz*
a lot/a little	*viel/wenig*
male/female	*männlich/weiblich*
near/far	*nah/weit*
old/new	*alt/neu*
old/young	*alt/jung*
smart/stupid	*klug/dumm*
smooth/rough	*glatt/rauh*
to ask/to answer	*fragen/antworten*
to break/to repair	*brechen/reparieren*
to give/to take	*geben/nehmen*
to laugh/to cry	*lachen/weinen*
to live/to die	*leben/sterben*

English Pair	German Pair
to love/to hate	lieben/hassen
to marry/to divorce	heiraten/scheiden
to shout/to whisper	schreien/flüstern
to sit/to stand	sitzen/stehen

To use any of the adjectives above in a simple sentence is easy: *Vater ist hungrig.* (Father is hungry.) However, if you place an adjective before a noun, it will require an ending, depending on the case and gender of the noun it is modifying: *Der hungrige Mann ist sehr krank.* (The hungry man is very sick.) Before you can figure out what adjective ending a word takes, you have to understand the difference between two types of identifying adjectives— *der* words and *ein* words.

Der Words and *ein* Words

Der words are the definite articles (*der, die, das*) and any other adjectives that act like definite articles with nouns. They are called demonstrative adjectives.

Der Words
- *dieser* (this)
- *jeder* (each)
- *jener* (that)
- *mancher* (many a)
- *solcher* (such)
- *welcher* (which)

You already know the *ein* words: *ein, kein, mein, dein, sein, ihr, unser, euer, Ihr,* and *ihr.*

These words indicate the gender and case of a noun. But you need to compare these two groups of words in order to use adjective endings more accurately. To generalize, you can say that the most common adjective ending in German is *–en*. But when is an adjective ending something other than *–en?*

Der Words

The nominative case (subject of the sentence) is the critical area. In this case the gender of the noun has to be specified. When you use a definite article, that becomes quite clear: *der Lehrer, die Lehrerin, das Kind.* And when you use an adjective with the definite articles, it always has an *–e* ending in the nominative: *der gute Lehrer* (the good teacher), *die nette Lehrerin* (the nice teacher), *das intelligente Kind* (the intelligent child).

No matter which *der* word you use, the adjective ending will always be just an *–e* in the nominative case.

▶ *Der* **Words in the Nominative Case**

Masculine	Feminine	Neuter
dieser alte Mann (this old man)	*diese alte Frau* (this old woman)	*dieses nette Kind* (this nice child)
jeder blaue Teller (each blue plate)	*jede blaue Tasse* (each blue cup)	*jedes blaue Glas* (each blue glass)
jener junge Lehrer (that young teacher)	*jene junge Lehrerin* (that young teacher)	*jenes hübsche Mädchen* (that pretty girl)
mancher gute Mann (many a good man)	*manche gute Frau* (many a good woman)	*manches gute Kind* (many a good child)

Since the feminine and neuter are identical in the nominative and accusative cases, you can assume that the same endings will apply in the accusative.

Ein *Words*

With *ein* words, gender is shown as an adjective ending, rather than by the article. The final sound of the definite article (*der, die, das*) appears as the adjective ending: *ein guter Mann, eine gute Frau, ein gutes Kind.* Let's look at some further examples.

▶ *Ein* Words in the Nominative Case

Masculine	Feminine	Neuter
sein neuer Wagen (his new car)	*seine neue Lampe* (his new lamp)	*sein neues Haus* (his new house)
unser junger Freund (our young friend)	*unsere junge Freundin* (our young friend)	*unser altes Buch* (our old book)
Ihr roter Hut (your red hat)	*Ihre rote Jacke* (your red jacket)	*Ihr rotes Hemd* (your red shirt)

Once again, the feminine and neuter would be identical in the accusative case.

If you understand this idea of gender being shown in the *der* word when using *der* words but gender being shown in the adjective when using *ein* words, then you know German adjectives. All other adjectives that follow *der* or *ein* words will end in *–en.* Let's take a look at that.

▶ *Der* Words and *Ein* Words in All Cases

Case	Masculine	Feminine	Neuter	Plural
Nom.	*dieser nette Freund*	*diese nette Freundin*	*dieses nette Kind*	*diese netten Kinder*
Nom.	*sein netter Freund*	*seine nette Freundin*	*sein nettes Kind*	*seine netten Kinder*
Acc.	*diesen netten Freund*	*diese nette Freundin*	*dieses nette Kind*	*diese netten Kinder*

Case	Masculine	Feminine	Neuter	Plural
Acc.	*seinen netten Freund*	*seine nette Freundin*	*sein nettes Kind*	*seine netten Kinder*
Dat.	*diesem netten Freund*	*dieser netten Freundin*	*diesem netten Kind*	*diesen netten Kindern*
Dat.	*seinem netten Freund*	*seiner netten Freundin*	*seinem netten Kind*	*seinen netten Kindern*
Gen.	*dieses netten Freundes*	*dieser netten Freundin*	*dieses netten Kindes*	*dieser netten Kinder*
Gen.	*seines netten Freundes*	*seiner netten Freundin*	*seines netten Kindes*	*seiner netten Kinder*

Adjectives of plural nouns, whether used with *der* words or *ein* words, have an *–en* ending in all cases: nominative, accusative, dative, and genitive.

Making Comparisons

When you use an adjective, you make a judgment or give an opinion about size, color, or quality of something. But when you want to compare two persons or things, you have to know the "comparative" form of the adjective.

That's not as complicated as it sounds. When you make a judgment or express an opinion using a comparative adjective, you decide which of two things has more or less of the quality in question. Forming English comparative adjectives is relatively easy: Just add *–er* to the adjective. There are a few spelling rules to worry about, but, in general, most comparative adjectives follow the same pattern: big/bigger.

But longer adjectives—adjectives that come to English from a Latin source—do not add *–er* to form the comparative. Instead, you place the word "more" in front of the adjective: interesting/more interesting. English also has a few irregular comparative forms: good/better.

German is much the same. The comparative of most adjectives is formed by adding *–er* to the adjective.

▶ Comparative Endings to German Adjectives

Adjective	+ –er	English
interessant	interessanter	more interesting
komisch	komischer	funnier
laut	lauter	louder
reich	reicher	richer
schön	schöner	nicer

Notice that longer words in German still form their comparative meaning by adding *–er* (*interessanter*) and do not require a different formation like English (more interesting).

Adjectives with an Umlaut vowel (*a, o, u*) and that are composed of only one syllable tend to add an Umlaut in the comparative too.

- *alt*   *älter*   older
- *arm*   *ärmer*   poorer
- *groß*   *größer*   bigger

If the adjective ends in *–er* or *–el*, you drop the *–e* when you add the comparative ending.

- *sauer*   *saurer*   sourer
- *dunkel*   *dunkler*   darker

When you want to show an "equality" between two things or persons, you can use the phrase *so . . . wie . . .* (as . . . as . . .). In this phrase the adjective will not require an adjective ending and is not changed to its comparative form.

■   *groß*   *Hans ist so groß wie sein Bruder.*
     (Hans is as big as his brother.)

Using in a Comparison

When you compare two things and judge one to be of a greater or lesser degree of a certain quality, you use *als* (than) with the comparative adjective. The same will be true if you use a comparative adverb. In these cases, like the examples above, there is no need for an adjective ending.

■   *groß*   *Unser Haus ist größer als euer Haus.*
     (Our house is bigger than your house.)

Just like English, German has a few peculiar forms to worry about. Just as "good" becomes "better" in English, the adjective *gut* changes to *besser* in the German comparative. There are a few others to think about:

■   *gut/besser   Er spielt besser als ich.*
     (He plays better than me.)
■   *bald/eher or früher   Wir fahren früher.*
     (We're leaving [driving] earlier.)
■   *gern/lieber   Hans spielt lieber Schach.*
     (Hans prefers to play chess.)
■   *hoch/höher   Der Wolkenkratzer ist höher als die Kirche.*
     (The skyscraper is taller [higher] than the church.)
■   *viel/mehr   Sie haben mehr Zeit als wir.*
     (They have more time than we do.)

Good ... Better ... Best

Now that you know the comparative form of adjectives, it's time to learn the superlative degree. The superlative is used to show the person or thing that has the greatest or least degree of a certain quality. In English it is formed by adding *–est* to the adjective or adverb: tall, taller, tallest. Or by using the word "most" with longer adjectives: interesting, more interesting, most interesting.

German is similar. You form the German superlative by adding *–st* to an adjective or adverb.

▶ **Forming the Superlative**

Adjective	+ –st	English
klein	kleinst	smallest
schön	schönst	nicest
langsam	langsamst	slowest

If the adjective ends in *–d, –t, –s, –ss, –ß,* or *–z,* add an *–e* before putting on the superlative ending. Notice also that the short adjectives also take Umlauts over the letters *a, o,* or *u,* just as in the comparative.

But the superlative adjective is a modifier and requires an ending. When it is a predicative adjective (standing alone at the end of a phrase) or an adverb, it is preceded by the preposition *am: am kleinsten* (the littlest), *am ältesten* (the oldest), *am schönsten* (the nicest).

There are a few irregular superlatives that you should also know.

▶ **Irregular Superlatives**

Positive	Comparative	Superlative	English
groß	größer	am größten	biggest
gut	besser	am besten	best

Positive	Comparative	Superlative	English
hoch	*höher*	*am höchsten*	highest
nah	*näher*	*am nächsten*	nearest
viel	*mehr*	*am meisten*	most

When the comparative or superlative adjective modifies a noun directly, it requires an adjective ending like any other adjective. Remember that the form *am kleinsten* is used as a predicate adjective. For example: *Das ist eine gute Idee!* (That's a good idea.) vs. *Das ist eine bessere Idee!* (That's a better idea.) vs. *Das ist die beste Idee!* (That's the best idea.)

Conjunctions: Ifs, Ands, and Buts

A word that connects two or more clauses is a conjunction. You encountered the conjunctions *und* and *oder* in previous chapters. *Und* (and) lets you combine two or more ideas: The boy **and** the girl. Tom is working in the kitchen, **and** Bill is working in the garage. *Oder* (or) tells you what options you have: A book **or** a magazine. You can sleep in the attic, **or** you can sleep on the floor.

The conjunction *aber* (but) puts two ideas together, but it shows a contrast: It's sunny, **but** a storm is brewing. She was very happy, **but** tears streamed down her face.

Some English conjunctions are "and," "but," "or," "because," "that," "if," "as if."

German conjunctions function in the same way, and many of them require no special rules for using them. *Und* (and), *aber* (but), *oder* (or), and *denn* (because) are four such conjunctions, and they put sentences together just like their English counterparts.

- *Sie ist krank. Ich rufe den Arzt an.*
  Sie ist krank, und ich rufe den Arzt an.
  (She is sick, and I call the doctor.)
- *Sie gibt ihm zwei Dollar. Er sagt nichts.*
  Sie gibt ihm zwei Dollar, aber er sagt nichts.
  (She gives him two dollars, but he says nothing.)
- *Ich schlafe bis zehn. Ich gehe spät ins Bett.*
  Ich schlafe bis zehn, denn ich gehe spät ins Bett.
  (I sleep until ten because I go to bed late.)
- *Kannst du hier bleiben?*
  Musst du schon nach Hause gehen?
  Kannst du hier bleiben oder musst du schon nach Hause gehen? (Can you stay here or must you go home already?)

You'll notice that each of these conjunctions combines two complete sentences. Each one has a subject and a verb, and, just like other sentences with normal word order, the subject comes before the verb in each. However, there are other conjunctions that require a change in the order of the sentence.

Conjunctions That Affect Word Order

German has other conjunctions that are important to know and are used very frequently in the language. Four of these are *dass* (that), *weil* (because), *wenn* (whenever or if), and *als* (when). They act like the other German conjunctions and combine sentences and clauses. But these four are special. When they're used in a sentence, the conjugated verb has to be placed at the very end of the clause in which the conjunction occurs. For example: *Ich wusste nicht, dass du Österreicher bist.* (I didn't know that you are an Austrian.).

Both *denn* and *weil* mean "because." *Denn* follows the rules of normal word order. *Weil* requires the verb at the end of the clause:

■ *Sie ist traurig, denn ihr Vater ist gestorben.* (She is sad because her father died.)
■ *Sie ist traurig, weil ihr Vater gestorben ist.* (She is sad because her father died.)

When you wish to convey the meaning of "whenever," use *wenn.* The conjunction *als* means "when" in the past tense. For example: *Wenn ich in Berlin bin, besuche ich meine Tante.* (Whenever I'm in Berlin, I visit my aunt.) *Als ich in Berlin war, besuchte ich meine Tante.* (When I was in Berlin, I visited my aunt.)

Interrogatives Used as Conjunctions

Besides asking questions, the interrogatives can be used to combine two sentences, often acting as the response to a question: "Who took the newspaper?" "I don't know who took the newspaper."

The German interrogatives function in the same way. The only difference is that when they're used in an indirect response, the conjugated verb becomes the last element in the sentence. For example: *Wer ist im Garten? Ich weiß nicht, wer im Garten ist.* (I don't know who's in the garden.)

You probably noticed that *wann* is the third German word you've learned that can mean "when." Just remember that *wann* is used to ask questions, *wenn* is used for the meaning "whenever," and *als* means "when" in the past tense.

05 / Getting Around

Securing a Room

If you're touring Germany, you're not going to want to spend the night on a park bench or curled up in a corner somewhere in an airport. There are always comfortable places to stay with a variety of price ranges throughout the country. Tourism is a big industry in Germany, so a lot of effort goes into providing suitable accommodations for visitors.

The word *Hotel* denotes exactly what it sounds like. This is an obvious place to stay. But just like in the United States, German hotels run the gamut of price range, facilities, and quality. If you're looking for luxury, it's there for you. If you want a cheap place to lay your head for the night, you'll find that, too.

But besides *das Hotel,* there are other places to spend the night, such as an inn. They can be called *Gaststätte, Gasthaus,* or *Gasthof.* And in many places, little villages or big cities, you can find a bed-and-breakfast: *Zimmer frei.* And if you're young at heart, a *Jugendherberge* (youth hostel) is a very inexpensive option.

▶ What You Can Expect in a German Hotel

German Name	English Name
der Aufzug	elevator
das Badetuch	bath towel
die Badewanne	bathtub
die Bettdecke	blanket
die Dusche	shower
das Fax	fax
der Fernseher	TV
der Geldautomat	ATM
der Gepäckträger	porter
die Halbpension	breakfast included
das Handtuch	hand towel
das Kissen	pillow
der Parkplatz	parking lot
der Pförtner	porter, doorkeeper
die Rezeption	reception desk
die Reinigung	cleaners
das Restaurant	restaurant
die Rolltreppe	escalator
der Schlüssel	key
das Schwimmbad	swimming pool
die Toilette	bathroom
die Vollpension	all meals included
die Wechselstube	money exchange office
das Zimmermädchen	maid

When checking in at *die Rezeption,* you ask, *"Haben Sie ein Zimmer frei?"* ("Do you have a room available?") You can specify *Doppelzimmer* or *Einzelzimmer* (a double or a single room). If you're bringing along your computer or electric shaver or hair dryer, you might request an *Adapter,* if you haven't brought your own along. Germany,

like all of Europe, is on 220 volts, not 110 volts like the
United States.

Around the House

An interesting category of vocabulary words has to do
with the home, household objects, and furniture. You can
use these to talk about what's in your house and what goes
on inside your four walls. Look at the words listed below
and practice using them in sentences you already know.

▶ *Eigner Herd ist Goldes Wert.* (There's no place like home.)

German Phrase	English
aufmachen	to open
aufschließen	to unlock
baden	to take a bath
die Badewanne	bathtub
das Badezimmer	bathroom
der Bücherschrank	bookcase
das Dach	roof
der Dachziegel	roof tile
die Dachstube	attic
die Decke	ceiling
die Dusche	shower
duschen	to take a shower
das Esszimmer	dining room
das Fenster	window
die Fliese	(floor) tile
der Fußboden	floor
der Herd	kitchen range
der Kamin	fireplace
die Küche	kitchen

German Phrase	English
der Kühlschrank	refrigerator
die Lampe	lamp
der Ofen	oven
das Schlafzimmer	bedroom
das Schloss und der Schlüssel	lock and key
hinter Schloss und Riegel	behind lock and key
der Schornstein	chimney
der Schrank	closet
das Sofa	sofa, couch
der Spiegel	mirror
die Stehlampe	floor lamp
der Stuhl	chair
die Terrasse	terrace
der Tisch	table
den Tisch abräumen	to clear the table
den Tisch decken	to set the table
am Tisch sitzen	to sit at the table
die Treppe	stairway
die Tür	door
die Wand	wall
das Wohnzimmer	living room
der Zaun	fence
zumachen	to close
zuschließen	to lock

Kaffee und Kuchen

Did you know that late afternoon is one of the most pleasant times in Germany? That's when families and friends sit down for *Kaffee und Kuchen* (coffee and cake).

Most families actually serve more than just coffee. Depending on the region in Germany and the time of year, you'll find tea, beer, wine, and various soft drinks on the table. A special treat is a *Bowle*—a punch often filled with fresh fruit.

The pastries served can be just as varied. If *Mutti* hasn't baked them herself, they were probably just brought in from a local *Konditorei*. Here are just some of the things you'll find on the table:

▶ **The Goodies for *Kaffee und Kuchen***

German Names	English Translation
Kaffee mit Zucker	coffee with sugar
Kaffee mit Sahne	coffee with cream
Tee mit Zucker	tea with sugar
Tee mit Honig	tea with honey
Limonade	lemonade
Schokoladenmilch	chocolate milk
Plätzchen	cookies
Apfelkuchen	apple cake (tart)
Obsttorte	fruit torte
Pflaumentorte	plum torte
Pfirsichtorte	peach torte
Eis	ice cream
Schlagsahne	whipped cream

When you're in Germany, don't miss the event. If you can't enjoy it with a family, go to a *Konditorei*. *Guten Appetit!* Enjoy your food!

Modern Times and Technology in Germany

You already know many words that are the same in both German and English. But here's a special category of words that deal with modern technology. They're mostly English words, picked up by Germans without changes, but to use them in German, you need to know their gender if they're nouns and their conjugation if they're verbs.

- *die Hotline: Rufen Sie unsere Hotline an!* (Call our hotline.)
- *faxen: Ich möchte etwas faxen.* (I'd like to fax something.)
- *das Fax: Ich bekam ein Fax von ihm.* (I got a fax from him.)
- *das Internet: Das Internet wird immer wichtiger.* (The Internet is getting more and more important.)
- *der Benutzername: Was ist Ihr Benutzername?* (What's your username?)
- *das Passwort: Hast du kein Passwort?* (Don't you have a password?)
- *klicken: Klicken Sie auf eine Kategorie!* (Click on a category.)
- *der Chat-Raum: Dieser Chat-Raum ist dumm.* (This chat-room is stupid.)
- *chatten: Ich kann nicht lange chatten.* (I can't chat for long.)
- *das Domain: Was ist der Domain Name?* (What's the domain name?)
- *die Mail: Ich habe wieder Mail.* (I've got mail again.)
- *die E-Mail: Ich bekam keine E-Mail.* (I didn't get any e-mail.)
- *der Download: Der Download wird zehn Minuten dauern.* (The download will take ten minutes.)
- *online: Ich habe es online bestellt.* (I ordered it online.)
- *der Laserdrucker: Wir haben jetzt einen Laserdrucker in unserem Büro.* (We now have a laser printer in our office.)

- *die DVD: Er hat viele DVDs.* (He has a lot of DVDs.)
- *die CD: Wir haben keine CDs. (*We don't have any CDs.)
- *das Video: Das Video dauert zwei Stunden.* (The video lasts for two hours.)
- *der Scanner: Ich soll einen neuen Scanner kaufen.* (I should buy a new scanner.)
- *der Chip: Jetzt ist der Chip verdorben.* (The chip is ruined now.)

Games and Sports

Did you know that Germans are into fitness and athletics just like Americans? They love games and sports. Not surprisingly, many German words for games and sports are taken directly from English. The list below gives some popular sports along with a sentence that you might hear in a conversation.

- *Basketball* (or *Korbball*): *Er spielt gern Basketball.* (He likes playing basketball.)
- *Fahrrad fahren: Wo fahren Sie Fahrrad?* (Where do you go bike riding?)
- *Fußball: Karl spielt gut Fußball.* (Karl plays soccer well.)
- *Golf: Golf ist mein Lieblingssport.* (Golf is my favorite sport.)
- *Handball: Wo spielt ihr Handball?* (Where do you play handball?)
- *joggen: Ich möchte gern joggen.* (I'd like to go jogging.)
- *Karten: Die Jungen spielen Karten.* (The boys are playing cards.)

■ *Schach: Sabine spielt gern Schach.* (Sabine likes to play chess.)

■ *Schlittschuh laufen: Wir gehen Schlittschuh laufen.* (We're going ice skating.)

■ *schwimmen: Schwimmst du gern?* (Do you like swimming?)

■ *Ski laufen: Wir gehen Ski laufen.* (We're going skiing.)

■ *Tennis: Wir spielen gern Tennis.* (We like playing tennis.)

■ *Tischtennis: Er möchte gern Tischtennis spielen.* (He'd like to play Ping-Pong.)

A Love for Animals
An interesting category of words is animals and birds. Whether domestic or exotic, you'll find many animal names in German similar to English. Let's take a look.

▶ *Tiere und Vögel* (Animals and Birds)

German	English
der Adler	eagle
der Affe	ape, monkey
der Bär	bear
der Elch	elk
der Elefant	elephant
die Ente	duck
der Fuchs	fox
die Gans	goose
der Geier	vulture
die Giraffe	giraffe
der Gorilla	gorilla

German	English
das Huhn	chicken
der Jaguar	jaguar
die Kuh	cow
der Löwe	lion
das Pferd	horse
das Reh	deer
das Schaf	sheep
der Schimpanse	chimpanzee
die Schlange	snake
der Schwan	swan
das Schwein	pig
der Seehund	seal
die Seemöwe	seagull
der Stier	bull
das Stinktier	skunk
die Taube	pigeon, dove
der Tiger	tiger
der Wal(fisch)	whale
das Walross	walrus
der Wolf	wolf
die Ziege	goat

Paying with the Euro

Most of continental Europe is using the *Euro* as its official currency. That includes Germany. The German Mark (its symbol is *DM*) is no longer in use. There are 100 *Cent* in approximately one *Euro,* which corresponds easily to 100 cents in a dollar, and which makes understanding European money quite simple. Compare the following:

▶ Dollars and *Euros*

American Dollars and Cents	European Euro and Cent
$5.50	5,50 EUR
$10.95	10,95 EUR
$1.25	1,25 EUR

Prices are said with the *Euro* amount first and followed by the number of *Cent*. For 6,10 EUR and 2,05 EUR you would say *"Sechs Euro und zehn Cent"* and *"Zwei Euro und fünf Cent."*

Be aware that sometimes the letters EUR stand in front of the figure and sometimes behind it. You'll encounter both: EUR 3,15 and 3,15 EUR. It may also appear with the symbol €: **3,15 €.**

You can ask how much something costs by asking, *Wie viel kostet das?* (How much does that cost?) The reply might be something like, *Das kostet zwei Euro und fünf Cent.*

Appendix A / German to English Dictionary

*Note that German nouns are followed by the following abbreviations: "m." stands for masculine (*der*), "f." stands for feminine (*die*), "n." stands for neuter (*das*), and "pl." stands for plural *(die).*

abfahren	to depart
abhauen	to get out
abholen	to pick up
Abitur machen	to make the Abitur, graduate
abräumen	to clear (the table)
acht	eight
Achtung, f.	attention
achtzehn	eighteen
achtzig	eighty
Adler, m.	eagle
Affe, m.	ape, monkey
alle	everyone, all
allein	alone
alles	everything, all
Alpen, pl.	Alps

als	as, when, than
als ob	as if
als wenn	as if
Alte, m.	old man
altmodisch	old-fashioned
Aluminium, n.	aluminum
Amerikaner, m.	American
an	at
ankommen	to arrive
annehmen	to assume
anprobieren	to try on
anrufen	to call up
Ansichtskarte, f.	picture postcard
anstatt	instead of
antworten	to answer
Apfel, m.	apple
Apfelkuchen, m.	apple cake, tort
April, m.	April
Arbeit, f.	work
arbeiten	to work
arm	poor
Armbanduhr, f.	wristwatch
Arzt, m.	physician
auch	also, too
auf Wiederhören	good-bye (on the phone)
auf Wiedersehen	good-bye
auf	on, onto
aufhören	to stop, cease
aufmachen	to open
aufschlagen	to open (a book)
aufschließen	to unlock
aufstehen	to stand up, get up

Augen, f.	eyes
August, m.	August
aus	from, out of
ausgeben	to spend (money)
Ausländer, m.	foreigner
Auslandsgespräch, n.	overseas call
außer	except
Ausstellung, f.	exhibition
Austauschschüler, m.	exchange student
Autobahn, f.	super highway
Autounfall, m.	car accident
backen	to bake
Bäcker, m.	baker
Bäckerei, f.	bakery
Badezimmer, n.	bathroom
Badewanne, f.	bathtub
Bahnhof, m.	railroad station
Bahnsteig, m.	platform
Ballonfahren	hot-air ballooning
Bär, m.	bear
Bart, m.	beard
Bauernhof, m.	farm
Bayern	Bavaria
bei	at, by, at the house of
beibringen	to teach
Bein, n.	leg
beinahe	almost
bekommen	to receive, get
Belgien	Belgium
berühmt	famous
besetzt	busy, occupied
besser	better

bestehen (aus)	to consist (of)
bestellen	to order
bestrafen	to punish
besuchen	to visit
Bett, n.	bed
Bibliothek, f.	library
Bier, n.	beer
Billion, f.	trillion
bis	until, as far as
bitte	please
bitten	to ask, request, beg
bitte schön	you're welcome
blau	blue
Blei, n.	lead
bleiben	to stay, remain
Bleistift, m.	pencil
blind	blind
Blume, f.	flower
Bluse, f.	blouse
Boden, m.	floor
Botschaft, f.	message, embassy
brauchen	to need
braun	brown
brechen	to break
Brief, m.	letter
Brille, f.	(eye)glasses
Brot, n.	bread
Brötchen, n.	bread roll
Brücke, f.	bridge
Brunnen, m.	well
Brust, f.	chest
Buch, n.	book

Bücherschrank, m.	bookcase
Bundestag, m.	parliament
Büro, n.	office
Bus, m.	bus
Busen, m.	bosom
Butter, f.	butter
Café, n.	café
Dach, n.	roof
Dachstube, f.	attic
Dachziegel, m.	roof tile
Dame, f.	lady
danken	to thank
danke schön	thank you
Datum, n.	date
Daumen, m.	thumb
Decke, f.	ceiling
dein	your
denken	to think
denn	because, then
Deutschland	Germany
Dezember, m.	December
Dieb, m.	thief
Dienstag, m.	Tuesday
dieser	this
Diskothek, f.	discotheque
Donnerstag, m.	Thursday
Dorf, n.	village
dort	there
Drachenfliegen	hang-gliding
drei	three
dreißig	thirty
dreizehn	thirteen

dritte	third
du	you (informal)
dumm	stupid
Dummheit, f.	stupidity
dunkel	dark
durch	through
dürfen	may, to be permitted
Dusche, f.	shower
ebenso	just as
Ecke, f.	corner
Ehefrau, f.	wife
eher	sooner, earlier
Eigentum, n.	property
Einbahnstraße, f.	one-way street
einfach	simple, single
Einigkeit, f.	unity
Einkommen, n.	income
einmal	once, one time
eins	one
Einsamkeit, f.	loneliness
einschlafen	to fall asleep
Eis, n.	ice, ice cream
Eisen, m.	iron
Eisenbahn, f.	railroad
Eisenbahnwagen, m.	railroad car
Elch, m.	elk
Elefant, m.	elephant
elf	eleven
Ellenbogen, m.	elbow
Eltern, pl.	parents
empfinden	to perceive
energisch	energetic

Engländer, m.	Englishman
Enkel, m.	grandson
Ente, f.	duck
entlassen	to dismiss, release
er, m.	he, it
Erkältung, f.	cold
erschlagen	to kill, strike dead
erste	first
erwarten	to expect, await
es, n.	it
es gibt	there is, there are
essen	to eat
Essen, n.	food
Eßzimmer, n.	dining room
etwas	something
Fabel, f.	fable
fahren	to drive
Fahrrad, n.	bike
fallen	to fall
Familie, f.	family
fangen	to catch
faul	lazy
Februar, m.	February
Feld, n.	field
Fenster, n.	window
Ferngespräch, n.	long-distance call
fernsehen	to watch TV
Fernseher, m.	TV set
finden	to find
Finger, m.	finger
Firma, f.	company
Flasche, f.	bottle

Fleischer, m.	butcher
fleißig	diligent
fliegen	to fly
Fliese, f.	floor tile
Flughafen, m.	airport
Flugkarte, f.	airline ticket
Flugzeug, n.	airplane
flüstern	to whisper
folgen	to follow
fragen	to ask (a question)
Franzose, m.	Frenchman
Frau, f.	woman, Mrs., Ms.
Fräulein, n.	Miss
Freitag, m.	Friday
Freund, m.	friend
Freundin, f.	girlfriend
Fröhlichkeit, f.	joyfulness
früh	early
Frühling, m.	spring
Fuchs, m.	fox
fünf	five
fünfzehn	fifteen
fünfzig	fifty
für	for
furchtbar	terrible
Fuß, m.	foot
Fußball, m.	soccer
Fußboden, m.	floor
Gans, f.	goose
ganz	whole
gar nichts	nothing at all
Garten, m.	garden

geben	to give
geboren	born
gebrauchen	to use
Geburtstag, m.	birthday
gefallen	to please
gegen	against
gehen	to go
gehören	to belong to
Geier, m.	vulture
Geigenspieler, m.	violinist
Gelächter, n.	laughter
gelb	yellow
Geld, n.	money
Gemüse, n.	vegetables
genau	exactly
genug	enough
gerne	gladly
gern haben	to like
geschehen	to occur, happen
Geschenk, n.	gift
Geschmack, m.	taste, flavor
Geschwister, pl.	siblings, brothers and sisters
Gespenst, n.	ghost
gesund	well, healthy
Gesundheit, f.	health
geteilt durch	divided by
Getreide, n.	grain
Gewicht, n.	weight
gewinnen	to win, gain
Gewitter, n.	thunderstorm
Giraffe, f.	giraffe
Gitarre, f.	guitar

Glas, n.	glass
glatt	smooth
glauben	to believe
gleich	equal, all the same
Gleitschirmfliegen	paragliding
Glück, n.	luck, fortune
Gold, n.	gold
Gorilla, m.	gorilla
Grad, m.	degree
Gramm, n.	gram
grau	gray
groß	big
Großmutter, f.	grandmother
Großvater, m.	grandfather
grün	green
gut	good, well
guten appetit	have a good meal
gute Reise	have a good trip
Gymnasium, n.	prep school
Haar, n.	hair
halb	half
Hälfte, f.	half
hallo	hey, hello
Hals, m.	neck, throat
Hand, f.	hand
Hase, m.	hare
hassen	to hate
hässlich	ugly
Hauptstadt, f.	capital city
Haus, n.	house
Hausaufgabe, f.	homework
Heft, n.	notebook

heilig	holy
heiraten	to marry
heiß	hot
heißen	to be called
helfen	to help
hell	bright, light
Hemd, n.	shirt
Herbst, m.	fall, autumn
Herd, m.	kitchen range
Herr, m.	man, Mr., gentleman
herrlich	terrific, glorious
heute	today
hier	here
Hilfe, f.	help, aid
hin und wieder	now and then
hinlegen	to put down
hinter	behind
hoch	high, tall
Hochdeutsch	High German
hoffentlich	hopefully
höher	higher, taller
holen	to get, fetch
Honig, m.	honey
hören	to hear, listen
Hose, f.	pants
hübsch	beautiful, handsome
Hüfte, f.	hip
Huhn, n.	chicken
hundert	hundred
hungrig	hungry
ich	I
Idee, f.	idea

Igel, m.	hedgehog
ihr	you (informal pl.)
ihr	her, their
Ihr	your (formal)
immer	always
in	in, into
interessant	interesting
Italien	Italy
Jacke, f.	jacket
Jaguar, m.	jaguar
Jahr, n.	year
Januar, m.	January
jeder	each
jener	that
jetzt	now
joggen	to jog
Jugend, f.	youth
Juli, m.	July
jung	young
Junge, m.	boy
Jüngling, m.	youngster
Juni, m.	June
Kaffee, m.	coffee
Käfig, m.	cage
Kaiser, m.	emperor
Kalender, m.	calendar
Kamin, m.	fireplace
Kämpe, m.	champion, warrior
kaputt	broken, wrecked
Käse, m.	cheese
kaufen	to buy
Kaufhaus, n.	department store

kein	no, not any
keine Ahnung	no idea
keinerlei	not any
keinesfalls	on no account
keineswegs	by no means
Keller, m.	cellar
kennen	to know, be acquainted
Kilometer, m.	kilometer
Kind, n.	child
Kindheit, f.	childhood
Kinn, n.	chin
Kino, n.	movie theater
Klapperschlange, f.	rattlesnake
Klasse, f.	class
Klavier, n.	piano
Kleid, n.	dress
klein	little
klug	smart, clever
Knabe, m.	boy, lad
Knie, n.	knee
Kolonie, f.	colony
komisch	funny, comical
kommen	to come
Konditorei, f.	pastry shop
König, m.	king
können	can, to be able
Konzert, n.	concert
Kopf, m.	head
Krähe, f.	crow
Kram, m.	mess
krank	sick
Krankenhaus, n.	hospital

Krankenpfleger, m.	male nurse
Krankenschwester, f.	nurse
Krankheit, f.	illness
Kreide, f.	chalk
Krieg, m.	war
Kronprinz, m.	crown prince
Küche, f.	kitchen
Kuh, f.	cow
kühl	cool
Kühlschrank, m.	refrigerator
Künstler, m.	artist
kurz	short
Kusine, f.	cousin
Küste, f.	coast
lachen	to laugh
Laden, m.	store, shop
Landschaft, f.	landscape
lang	long
langsam	slow
langweilig	boring
lassen	to let
laufen	to run
laut	loud, noisy
leben	to live
Lehrer, m.	teacher
Lehrling, m.	apprentice
leider	unfortunately
leise	quiet
Leiste, f.	groin
lernen	to learn
lesen	to read
letzte	last

German	English
Leute, pl.	people
lieben	to love
lieber	preferably
Löffel, m.	spoon
Lokal, n.	bar
Löwe, m.	lion
Luftschiff, n.	dirigible (Zeppelin)
machen	to do, make
mach's gut	take care, so long
Mädchen, n.	girl
Magen, m.	stomach
Mai, m.	May
Mal, n.	time, times
mancher	many a
männlich	masculine
Mantel, m.	coat
Markt, m.	market
März, m.	March
Matrose, m.	sailor
Meerschweinchen, n.	guinea pig
mehr	more
mein	my
meinen	to mean
Mensch, m.	man, human
Messing, n.	brass
Metzger, m.	butcher
Metzgerei, f.	butcher shop
Milch, f.	milk
Milliarde, f.	billion
Minute, f.	minute
mit	with
mitkommen	to come along

Mittag, m.	noon, midday
Mitternacht, f.	midnight
Mittwoch, m.	Wednesday
Mobiltelefon, n.	mobile phone, cell phone
modisch	fashionable
mögen	to like
Montag, m.	Monday
morgen	tomorrow
Morgen, m.	morning
müde	tired
Mund, m.	mouth
Münzeinwurf, m.	coin slot
Museum, n.	museum
Musik, f.	music
müssen	must, have to
Mutter, f.	mother
nach	after, to
nach Hause	home(ward)
Nachricht, f.	news, message
nachschlagen	to look up (in a book)
nächste	next
nah	near
Nase, f.	nose
Nashorn, n.	rhinoceros
naß	wet
Natur, f.	nature
natürlich	naturally
neben	next to
Neffe, m.	nephew
nehmen	to take
nervös	nervous
nett	nice

neu	new
Neuling, m.	novice
neun	nine
neunzehn	nineteen
neunzig	ninety
nicht	not
Nichte, f.	niece
nichtsdestoweniger	nonetheless
nie	never
Niedersachsen	Lower Saxony
niedrig	low
niemals	never
niemand	no one
Niemandsland	no man's land
Nilpferd, n.	hippo
nirgendwo	nowhere
noch	still, yet
November, m.	November
Null, f.	zero
nur	only
Obsttorte, f.	fruit torte
Ochse, m.	ox
oder	or
Ofen, m.	oven
ohne	without
Ohr, n.	ear
Oktober, m.	October
Oma, f.	grandma
Onkel, m.	uncle
Opa, m.	grandpa
Oper, f.	opera
Ortsgespräch, n.	local call

Österreich	Austria
Papier, n.	paper
Park, m.	park
passieren	to happen
Passwort, n.	password
perfekt	perfect
Pfeife, f.	pipe
Pferd, n.	horse
Pflanze, f.	plant
Pfund, n.	pound, half a kilo
Plattdeutsch	Low German
Platz, m.	(market) square, theater seat
Poesie, f.	poetry
Polen	Poland
Polizist, m.	policeman
populär	popular
Post, f.	post office, postal system
Postkarte, f.	postcard
Preis, m.	price, prize
Prinzessin, f.	princess
Prüfung, f.	test
Qualität, f.	quality
Quatsch, m.	nonsense
Radio, n.	radio
rauchen	to smoke
Raucherabteil, n.	smoking compartment
rauh	rough
recht	right
Regen, m.	rain
regnen	to rain
regnerisch	rainy
Reh, n.	deer

reich	rich
Reich, n.	empire
Reichstag, m.	parliament building in Berlin
Reinheit, f.	purity
Reisebüro, n.	travel agency
Reiseplan, m.	itinerary
Rennwagen, m.	racing car
reparieren	to repair
Restaurant, n.	restaurant
Richter, m.	judge
richtig	correct, right
Roman, m.	novel
Rose, f.	rose
rot	red
Rücken, m.	back
ruhig	quiet, calm
Russin, f.	Russian woman
sagen	to say
Sahne, f.	cream
Salz und Pfeffer	salt and pepper
Samstag, m.	Saturday
Sänger, m.	singer
satt	full, satiated
Sattel, m.	saddle
Satz, m.	sentence
sauber	clean
sauer	sour
Schach spielen	to play chess
schade	too bad
Schaf, n.	sheep
Schauspiel, n.	play
Schauspieler, m.	actor

scheiden	to divorce
schicken	to send
Schimpanse, m.	chimpanzee
schlafen	to sleep
Schlafzimmer, n.	bedroom
Schlagsahne, f.	whipped cream
Schlange, f.	snake
schlecht	bad
Schlittschuh laufen	to ice skate
Schloß, n.	lock, palace
Schlüssel, m.	key
Schnee, m.	snow
schnell	fast
Schokolade, f.	chocolate
schon	already
Schornstein, m.	chimney
Schrank, m.	cupboard
schreiben	to write
schreien	to shout, scream
Schule, f.	school
Schüler, m.	pupil
Schuljahr, n.	school year
Schulter, f.	shoulder
schwach	weak
Schwager, m.	brother-in-law
Schwägerin, f.	sister-in-law
Schwan, m.	swan
schwarz	black
Schwarzwald, m.	the Black Forest
Schweden	Sweden
Schwein, n.	pig
Schweiz, f.	Switzerland

Schwester, f.	sister
Schwiegermutter, f.	mother-in-law
schwimmen	to swim
sechs	six
sechzehn	sixteen
sechzig	sixty
See, f.	sea
See, m.	lake
Seehund, m.	seal
Seemöwe, f.	seagull
Segelfliegen	flying gliders
sehen	to see
sehr	very
sein	his, its (poss. pronoun)
sein	to be
seit	since
senden	to send
September, m.	September
sich	reflexive "oneself"
sie (sing.)	she, it
sie (pl.)	they
Sie	you (formal)
sieben	seven
siebzehn	seventeen
siebzig	seventy
Silber, n.	silver
sitzen	to sit
Ski laufen	to ski
so	so, as
Sofa, n.	sofa, couch
Sohn, m.	son
solcher	such a

Soldat, m.	soldier
sollen	should, ought to
Sommer, m.	summer
Sonnabend, m.	Saturday
sonnig	sunny
Sonntag, m.	Sunday
Spanier, m.	Spaniard
spät	late
Speisekarte, f.	menu
Sperling, m.	sparrow
Spiegel, m.	mirror
Spiel, n.	game
spielen	to play
Sprache, f.	language
sprechen	to speak
Stadt, f.	city
Stahl, m.	steel
stark	strong
stehen bleiben	to remain standing
Stehlampe, f.	floor lamp
steigen	climb
Stellung, f.	position
Stempel, m.	stamp, seal
sterben	to die
Stier, m.	bull
Stimme, f.	voice
Stinktier, n.	skunk
Storch, m.	stork
Studium, n.	study
Stuhl, m.	chair
Stunde, f.	hour
Sturm, m.	storm

Suche, f.	search
suchen	to look for, seek
süß	sweet
Tag, m.	day
tagsüber	during the day
Tante, f.	aunt
Tasche, f.	pocket
Taschenuhr, f.	pocket watch
Tasse, f.	cup
Taube, f.	pigeon, dove
tausend	thousand
Tee, m.	tea
Telefonbuch, n.	telephone book
Telefonhörer, m.	receiver
telefonieren	to telephone
Telefonzelle, f.	telephone booth
Teller, m.	plate
Temperatur, f.	temperature
Teppich, m.	rug, carpet
Terrasse, f.	terrace
Theater, n.	theater
Theorie, f.	theory
Tiger, m.	tiger
Tischtennis spielen	to play Ping-Pong
Tochter, f.	daughter
toll	great, crazy
Tomaten, pl.	tomatoes
töten	to kill
tragen	to carry, wear
traurig	sad
treffen	to meet
Treppe, f.	stairs

trinken	to drink
trocken	dry
trotz	in spite of
Tschüß	bye, so long
Tür, f.	door
Türkei, f.	Turkey
über	over, above
übermorgen	day after tomorrow
Übersetzung, f.	translation
überwiegen	prevail
Übung, f.	exercise
Uhr, f.	clock
um	at, around
umbringen	to murder
Umgangssprache, f.	colloquial language
und	and
Universität, f.	university
unter	under
unterwegs	on the way
ursprünglich	original
verbergen (sich)	to hide
verbringen	to spend (time)
verdorben	ruined, spoiled
Vereinigten Staaten, pl.	United States
vergessen	to forget
verkaufen	to sell
verlieren	to lose
versuchen	to try
Verwandten, pl.	relatives
Vetter, m.	cousin
viel	much
vier	four

Viertel, n.	quarter
vierzehn	fourteen
vierzig	forty
von	from, of
vor	in front of, before
vor allen Dingen	above all
vorgestern	day before yesterday
Vormittag, m.	morning
Vorwahl, f.	area code
Wagen, m.	car
wählen	to dial, to select
während	during
Wahrheit, f.	truth
Wal(fisch), m.	whale
Walross, n.	walrus
Wand, f.	wall
Wanduhr, f.	wall clock
warm	warm
warten	to wait
warum	why
was	what
was für	what kind of
Wasser, n.	water
Wecker, m.	alarm clock
weder . . . noch	neither . . . nor
wegen	because of
weiblich	feminine
weil	because
Wein, m.	wine
weinen	to cry
weiß	white
welcher	which

wem	whom (dat.)
wen	whom (acc.)
wenig	little (amount)
wenn	when, whenever, if
wer	who
werden	to become, get, will, shall
wessen	whose
Wetter, n.	weather
Wetterbericht, m.	weather report
wichtig	important
wider	against
wie	how
wieder	again
wild	wild
Wind, m.	wind
Winter, m.	winter
wir	we
Wirtschaft, f.	economy
wissen	to know
Wissenschaft, f.	science
wo	where
Woche, f.	week
Wochenende, n.	weekend
woher	from where
wohin	where (to)
wohnen	to live, reside
Wohnung, f.	apartment
Wohnzimmer, n.	living room
Wolf, m.	wolf
Wolke, f.	cloud
wollen	to want
Wurst, f.	sausage

wütend	furious
Zahnarzt, m.	dentist
Zaun, m.	fence
Zaunkönig, m.	wren
Zehe, f.	toe
zehn	ten
Zeit, f.	time
Zeitschrift, f.	magazine
Zeitung, f.	newspaper
zeitweise	from time to time
zerbrechen	to break to bits
zerstören	to destroy
Ziege, f.	goat
Zinn, n.	tin
zu	to
zu Besuch	for a visit
Zug, m.	train
zu Hause	at home
zumachen	to close
zurück	back
zuschließen	to lock
zwanzig	twenty
zwei	two
zwischen	between
zwo	two, same as zwei
zwölf	twelve

Appendix B / English to German Dictionary

*Note that German nouns are followed by the follow-ing abbreviations: "m." stands for masculine (*der*), "f." stands for feminine (*die*), "n." stands for neuter (*das*), and "pl." stands for plural (*die*).

above all	vor allen Dingen
actor	Schauspieler, m.
after	nach
again	wieder
against	gegen, wider
airline ticket	Flugkarte, f.
airplane	Flugzeug, n.
airport	Flughafen, m.
alarm clock	Wecker, m.
almost	beinahe
alone	allein
Alps	Alpen, pl.
already	schon
also, too	auch
aluminum	Aluminium, n.
always	immer

American	Amerikaner, m.
and	und
answer	antworten
apartment	Wohnung, f.
ape, monkey	Affe, m.
apple	Apfel, m.
apple cake, tart	Apfelkuchen, m.
apprentice	Lehrling, m.
April	April, m.
area code	Vorwahl, f.
around	um
arrive	ankommen
artist	Künstler, m.
as, than	als
as if	als ob, als wenn
ask (a question)	fragen
ask, request	bitten
assume	annehmen
at	an
at, by, at the house of	bei
at home	zu Hause
attention	Achtung, f.
attic	Dachstube, f.
August	August, m.
aunt	Tante, f.
Austria	Österreich
autumn	Herbst, m.
back	Rücken, m.
back	zurück
bad	schlecht
bake	backen
baker	Bäcker, m.
bakery	Bäckerei, f.
bar	Lokal, n.
bathroom	Badezimmer, n.

bathtub	Badewanne, f.
Bavaria	Bayern
be	sein
bear	Bär, m.
beard	Bart, m.
beautiful	hübsch
be called	heißen
because	denn, weil
because of	wegen
become, get	werden
bed	Bett, n.
bedroom	Schlafzimmer, n.
beer	Bier, n.
behind	hinter
Belgium	Belgien
believe	glauben
belong	gehören
better	besser
between	zwischen
big	groß
bike	Fahrrad, n.
billion	Milliarde, f.
birthday	Geburtstag, m.
black	schwarz
Black Forest	Schwarzwald, m.
blind	blind
blouse	Bluse, f.
blue	blau
book	Buch, n.
bookcase	Bücherschrank, m.
boring	langweilig
born	geboren
bosom	Busen, m.
bottle	Flasche, f.
boy	Junge, m.

brass	Messing, n.
bread	Brot, n.
bread roll	Brötchen, n.
break	brechen
break to bits	zerbrechen
bridge	Brücke, f.
bright	hell
broken, wrecked	kaputt
brother-in-law	Schwager, m.
brothers and sisters	Geschwister, pl.
brown	braun
bull	Stier, m.
bus	Bus, m.
busy, occupied	besetzt
butcher	Fleischer, m.
butcher	Metzger, m.
butcher shop	Metzgerei, f.
butter	Butter, f.
buy	kaufen
bye, so long	Tschüs
by no means	keineswegs
café	Café, n.
cage	Käfig, m.
calendar	Kalender, m.
call up	anrufen
calm, quiet	ruhig
can, be able	können
capital city	Hauptstadt, f.
car	Wagen, m.
car accident	Autounfall, m.
carry	tragen
catch	fangen
ceiling	Decke, f.
cellar	Keller, m.
chair	Stuhl, m.

chalk	Kreide, f.
champion, warrior	Kämpe, m.
cheese	Käse, m.
chest	Brust, f.
chicken	Huhn, n.
child	Kind, n.
childhood	Kindheit, f.
chimney	Schornstein, m.
chimpanzee	Schimpanse, m.
chin	Kinn, n.
chocolate	Schokolade, f.
city	Stadt, f.
class	Klasse, f.
clean	sauber
clear (the table)	abräumen
climb	steigen
clock	Uhr, f.
close	zumachen
closet	Schrank, m.
cloud	Wolke, f.
coast	Küste, f.
coat	Mantel, m.
coffee	Kaffee, m.
coin slot	Münzeinwurf, m.
cold	Erkältung, f.
colloquial language	Umgangssprache, f.
colony	Kolonie, f.
come	kommen
come along	mitkommen
company	Firma, f.
concert	Konzert, n.
consist (of)	bestehen (aus)
cool	kühl
corner	Ecke, f.
correct	richtig

cousin	Kusine, f., Vetter, m.
cow	Kuh, f.
cream	Sahne, f.
crow	Krähe, f.
crown prince	Kronprinz, m.
cry	weinen
cup	Tasse, f.
dark	dunkel
date	Datum, n.
daughter	Tochter, f.
day	Tag, m.
day after tomorrow	übermorgen
day before yesterday	vorgestern
December	Dezember, m.
deer	Reh, n.
degree	Grad, m.
dentist	Zahnarzt, m.
depart	abfahren
department store	Kaufhaus, n.
destroy	zerstören
dial, select	wählen
die	sterben
diligent	fleißig
dining room	Eßzimmer, n.
dirigible (Zeppelin)	Luftschiff, n.
discotheque	Diskothek, f.
dismiss	entlassen
divided by	geteilt durch
divorce	scheiden
do, make	machen
door	Tür, f.
dress	Kleid n.
drink	trinken
drive	fahren
dry	trocken

duck	Ente, f.
during	während
during the day	tagsüber
each	jeder
eagle	Adler, m.
ear	Ohr, n.
early	früh
eat	essen
economy	Wirtschaft, f.
eight	acht
eighteen	achtzehn
eighty	achtzig
elbow	Ellenbogen, m.
elephant	Elefant, m.
eleven	elf
elk	Elch, m.
emperor	Kaiser, m.
empire	Reich, n.
energetic	energisch
Englishman	Engländer, m.
enough	genug
equal	gleich
everyone, all	alle
everything, all	alles
exactly	genau
except	außer
exchange student	Austauschschüler, m.
exercise	Übung, f.
exhibition	Ausstellung, f.
expect, await	erwarten
eyes	Augen, f.
fable	Fabel, f.
fall	fallen
fall asleep	einschlafen
family	Familie, f.

famous	berühmt
farm	Bauernhof, m.
fashionable	modisch
fast	schnell
February	Februar, m.
feminine	weiblich
fence	Zaun, m.
field	Feld, n.
fifteen	fünfzehn
fifty	fünfzig
find	finden
finger	Finger, m.
fireplace	Kamin, m.
first	erste
five	fünf
floor	Boden, m., Fußboden, m.
floor lamp	Stehlampe, f.
floor tile	Fliese, f.
flower	Blume, f.
fly	fliegen
flying gliders	Segelfliegen
follow	folgen
food	Essen, n.
foot	Fuß, m.
for	für
for a visit	zu Besuch
foreigner	Ausländer, m.
forget	vergessen
forty	vierzig
four	vier
fourteen	vierzehn
fox	Fuchs, m.
Frenchman	Franzose, m.
Friday	Freitag, m.
friend	Freund, m.

from, of	von
from, out of	aus
from time to time	zeitweise
from where	woher
fruit torte	Obsttorte, f.
full, satiated	satt
funny	lustig
furious	wütend
game	Spiel, n.
garden	Garten, m.
gentleman	Herr, m.
Germany	Deutschland
get, fetch	holen
get out	abhauen
ghost	Gespenst, n.
gift	Geschenk, n.
giraffe	Giraffe, f.
girl	Mädchen, n.
girlfriend	Freundin, f.
give	geben
gladly	gerne
glass	Glas, n.
glasses	Brille, f.
go	gehen
goat	Ziege, f.
gold	Gold, n.
good	gut
good-bye	auf Wiedersehen
good-bye (on the phone)	auf Wiederhören
goose	Gans, f.
gorilla	Gorilla, m.
grain	Getreide, n.
gram	Gramm, n.
grandfather	Großvater, m.
grandma	Oma, f.

grandmother	Großmutter, f.
grandpa	Opa, m.
grandson	Enkel, m.
gray	grau
great, crazy	toll
green	grün
groin	Leiste, f.
guitar	Gitarre, f.
hair	Haar, n.
half	halb
half	Hälfte, f.
hand	Hand, f.
handsome	hübsch
hang-gliding	Drachenfliegen
happen	geschehen
hare	Hase, m.
hate	hassen
have a good meal	guten appetit
he, it, m.	er
head	Kopf, m.
health	Gesundheit, f.
healthy	gesund
hear	hören
hedgehog	Igel, m.
help	helfen
help	Hilfe, f.
her	ihr
here	hier
hey, hello	hallo
hide	verbergen (sich)
high	hoch
higher	höher
High German	Hochdeutsch
hip	Hüfte, f.
hippo	Nilpferd, n.

his	sein
holy	heilig
home(ward)	nach Hause
homework	Hausaufgabe, f.
honey	Honig, m.
hopefully	hoffentlich
horse	Pferd, n.
hospital	Krankenhaus, n.
hot	heiß
hot-air ballooning	Ballonfahren
hour	Stunde, f.
house	Haus, n.
how	wie
human	Mensch, m.
hundred	hundert
hungry	hungrig
I	ich
ice, ice cream	Eis, n.
ice skate	Schlittschuh laufen
idea	Idee, f.
if	wenn
illness	Krankheit, f.
important	wichtig
in, into	in
income	Einkommen, n.
in front of, before	vor
in spite of	trotz
instead of	anstatt
interesting	interessant
iron	Eisen, n.
it	es, n.
Italy	Italien
itinerary	Reiseplan, m.
its	sein
jacket	Jacke, f.

jaguar	Jaguar, m.
January	Januar, m.
jog	joggen
joyfulness	Fröhlichkeit, f.
judge	Richter, m.
July	Juli, m.
June	Juni, m.
just as	ebenso
key	Schlüssel, m.
kill	erschlagen, töten
kilometer	Kilometer, m.
king	König, m.
kitchen	Küche, f.
kitchen range	Herd, m.
knee	Knie, n.
know	wissen
know, be acquainted	kennen
lad	Knabe, m.
lady	Dame, f.
lake	See, m.
landscape	Landschaft, f.
language	Sprache, f.
last	letzte
late	spät
laugh	lachen
laughter	Gelächter, n.
lazy	faul
lead	Blei, n.
learn	lernen
leg	Bein, n.
let	lassen
letter	Brief, m.
library	Bibliothek, f.
like	gern haben, mögen
lion	Löwe, m.

little	klein
little (amount)	wenig
live	leben
live, reside	wohnen
living room	Wohnzimmer, n.
local call	Ortsgespräch, n.
lock	Schloß, n.
lock	zuschließen
loneliness	Einsamkeit, f.
long	lang
long distance call	Ferngespräch, n.
look for	suchen
look up (in a book)	nachschlagen
lose	verlieren
loud	laut
love	lieben
low	niedrig
Lower Saxony	Niedersachsen
Low German	Plattdeutsch
luck	Glück, n.
magazine	Zeitschrift, f.
make the Abitur, graduate	Abitur machen
male nurse	Krankenpfleger, m.
man	Herr, m.
many a	mancher
March	März, m.
market	Markt, m.
market square	Platz, m.
marry	heiraten
masculine	männlich
may	dürfen
May	Mai, m.
mean	meinen
meet	treffen
menu	Speisekarte, f.

mess	Kram, m.
message	Botschaft, f.
midnight	Mitternacht, f.
milk	Milch, f.
minute	Minute, f.
mirror	Spiegel, m.
Miss	Fräulein, n.
mobile phone, cell phone	Mobiltelefon, n.
Monday	Montag, m.
money	Geld, n.
more	mehr
morning	Morgen, m., Vormittag, m.
mother	Mutter, f.
mother-in-law	Schwiegermutter, f.
mouth	Mund, m.
movie theater	Kino, n.
Mr.	Herr, m.
Mrs.	Frau, f.
Ms.	Frau, f.
much	viel
murder	umbringen
museum	Museum, n.
music	Musik, f.
must, have to	müssen
my	mein
naturally	natürlich
nature	Natur, f.
near	nah
neck, throat	Hals, m.
need	brauchen
neither ... nor	weder ... noch
nephew	Neffe, m.
nervous	nervös
never	niemals, nie
new	neu

news, message	Nachricht, f.
newspaper	Zeitung, f.
next	nächste
next to	neben
nice	nett
niece	Nichte, f.
nine	neun
nineteen	neunzehn
ninety	neunzig
no, not any	kein
no idea	keine Ahnung
no man's land	Niemandsland
nonetheless	nichtsdestoweniger
nonsense	Quatsch, m.
noon	Mittag, m.
no one	niemand
nose	Nase, f.
not	nicht
not any	keinerlei
notebook	Heft, n.
nothing at all	gar nichts
novel	Roman, m.
November	November, m.
novice	Neuling, m.
now	jetzt
now and then	hin und wieder
nowhere	nirgendwo
nurse	Krankenschwester, f.
occur	passieren
October	Oktober, m.
office	Büro, n.
old-fashioned	altmodisch
old man	Alte, m.
on, onto	auf
once, one time	einmal

one	eins
one-way street	Einbahnstraße, f.
only	nur
on no account	keinesfalls
on the way	unterwegs
open	aufmachen
open (a book)	aufschlagen
opera	Oper, f.
or	oder
order	bestellen
original	ursprünglich
oven	Ofen, m.
over, above	über
overseas call	Auslandsgespräch, n.
ox	Ochse, m.
palace	Schloß, n.
pants	Hose, f.
paper	Papier, n.
parents	Eltern, pl.
park	Park, m.
parliament	Bundestag, m.
parliament building	
in Berlin	Reichstag, m.
password	Passwort, n.
pastry shop	Konditorei, f.
pencil	Bleistift, m.
people	Leute, pl.
perceive	empfinden
perfect	perfekt
physician	Arzt, m.
piano	Klavier, n.
pick up	abholen
picture postcard	Ansichtskarte, f.
pig	Schwein, n.
pigeon, dove	Taube, f.

pipe	Pfeife, f.
plant	Pflanze, f.
plate	Teller, m.
platform	Bahnsteig, m.
play	Schauspiel, n.
play	spielen
play chess	Schach spielen
play Ping-Pong	Tischtennis spielen
please	bitte
please	gefallen
pocket	Tasche, f.
pocket watch	Taschenuhr, f.
poetry	Poesie, f.
Poland	Polen
policeman	Polizist, m.
poor	arm
popular	populär
porpoise	Delphin, m.
position	Stellung, f.
postcard	Postkarte, f.
post office, postal system	Post, f.
pound, half a kilo	Pfund, n.
preferably	lieber
prep school	Gymnasium, n.
prevail	überwiegen
price	Preis, m.
princess	Prinzessin, f.
prize	Preis, m.
property	Eigentum, n.
punish	bestrafen
pupil	Schüler, m.
purity	Reinheit, f.
put down	hinlegen
quality	Qualität, f.
quarter	Viertel, n.

quiet	leise
racecar	Rennwagen, m.
radio	Radio, n.
railroad	Eisenbahn, f.
railroad car	Eisenbahnwagen, m.
railroad station	Bahnhof, m.
rain	Regen, m., regnen
rainy	regnerisch
rattlesnake	Klapperschlange, f.
read	lesen
receive, get	bekommen
red	rot
refrigerator	Kühlschrank, m.
relatives	Verwandten, pl.
remain standing	stehen bleiben
repair	reparieren
restaurant	Restaurant, n.
rhinoceros	Nashorn, n.
rich	reich
right	recht
roof	Dach, n.
roof tile	Dachziegel, m.
rose	Rose, f.
rough	rauh
rug, carpet	Teppich, m.
ruined, spoiled	verdorben
run	laufen
Russian woman	Russin, f.
sad	traurig
saddle	Sattel, m.
sailor	Matrose, m.
salt and pepper	Salz und Pfeffer
Saturday	Sonnabend, m., Samstag, m.
sausage	Wurst, f.
say	sagen

school	Schule, f.
school year	Schuljahr, n.
science	Wissenschaft, f.
sea	See, f.
seagull	Seemöwe, f.
seal	Seehund, m.
search	Suche, f., suchen
see	sehen
sell	verkaufen
send	schicken, senden
sentence	Satz, m.
September	September, m.
seven	sieben
seventeen	siebzehn
seventy	siebzig
she	sie (singular)
sheep	Schaf, n.
shirt	Hemd, n.
short	kurz
should, ought to	sollen
shoulder	Schulter, f.
shout, scream	schreien
shower	Dusche, f., duschen
sick	krank
silver	Silber, n.
simple	einfach
since	seit
singer	Sänger, m.
sister	Schwester, f.
sister-in-law	Schwägerin, f.
sit	sitzen
six	sechs
sixteen	sechzehn
sixty	sechzig
ski	Ski laufen

skunk	Stinktier, n.
sleep	schlafen
slow	langsam
smart	klug
smoke	rauchen
smoking compartment	Raucherabteil, n.
smooth	glatt
snake	Schlange, f.
snow	Schnee, m.
soccer	Fußball, m.
sofa, couch	Sofa, n.
soldier	Soldat, m.
something	etwas
son	Sohn, m.
sooner	eher
sour	sauer
Spaniard	Spanier, m.
sparrow	Sperling, m.
speak	sprechen
spend (money)	ausgeben
spend (time)	verbringen
spoon	Löffel, m.
spring	Frühling, m.
stairs	Treppe, f.
stamp, seal	Stempel, m.
stand up, get up	aufstehen
stand	stehen
stay, remain	bleiben
steel	Stahl, m.
still	noch
stomach	Magen, m.
stop, cease	aufhören
store	Laden, m.
stork	Storch, m.
storm	Sturm, m.

strong	stark
study	Studium, n., studieren
stupid	dumm
stupidity	Dummheit, f.
such a	solcher
summer	Sommer, m.
Sunday	Sonntag, m.
sunny	sonnig
super highway	Autobahn, f.
swan	Schwan, m.
Sweden	Schweden
sweet	süß
swim	schwimmen
Switzerland	Schweiz, f.
take	nehmen
taste	Geschmack, m.
tea	Tee, m.
teach	beibringen
teacher	Lehrer, m.
telephone	telefonieren
telephone book	Telefonbuch, n.
telephone booth	Telefonzelle, f.
telephone operator	Vermittlung, f.
telephone receiver	Telefonhörer, m.
temperature	Temperatur, f.
ten	zehn
terrace	Terrasse, f.
terrible	furchtbar
terrific, glorious	herrlich
test	Prüfung, f.
thank	danken
thank you	danke schön
that	jener
theater	Theater, n.
theater seat	Platz, m.

their	ihr
theory	Theorie, f.
there	da
there	dort
there is, there are	es gibt
they	sie (plural)
thief	Dieb, m.
think	denken
third	dritte
thirteen	dreizehn
thirty	dreißig
this	dieser
thousand	tausend
three	drei
through	durch
thumb	Daumen, m.
thunderstorm	Gewitter, n.
Thursday	Donnerstag, m.
tiger	Tiger, m.
time	Mal, n., Zeit, f.
tin	Zinn, n.
tired	müde
to	zu
today	heute
toe	Zehe, f.
tomatoes	Tomaten, pl.
tomorrow	morgen
too bad	schade
train	Zug, m.
translation	Übersetzung, f.
travel agency	Reisebüro, n.
trillion	Billion, f.
truth	Wahrheit, f.
try	versuchen
try on	anprobieren

Tuesday	Dienstag, m.
Turkey	Türkei, f.
TV set	Fernseher, m.
twelve	zwölf
twenty	zwanzig
two	zwei, zwo
ugly	hässlich
uncle	Onkel, m.
under	unter
unfortunately	leider
United States	Vereinigten Staaten, pl.
unity	Einigkeit, f.
university	Universität, f.
unlock	aufschließen
until, as far as	bis
use	gebrauchen
vegetables	Gemüse, n.
very	sehr
village	Dorf, n.
violinist	Geigenspieler, m.
visit	besuchen
voice	Stimme, f.
vulture	Geier, m.
wait	warten
wall	Wand, f.
wall clock	Wanduhr, f.
walrus	Walross, n.
want	wollen
war	Krieg, m.
warm	warm
watch TV	fernsehen
water	Wasser, n.
we	wir
weak	schwach
wear	tragen

weather	Wetter, n.
weather report	Wetterbericht, m.
Wednesday	Mittwoch, m.
week	Woche, f.
weekend	Wochenende, n.
weight	Gewicht, n.
well	Brunnen, m.
well	gut
wet	naß
whale	Wal(fisch), m.
what	was
what kind of	was für
when, whenever	wenn
where	wo
where (to)	wohin
which	welcher
whipped cream	Schlagsahne, f.
whisper	flüstern
white	weiß
who	wer
whole	ganz
whom	wen, wem
whose	wessen
why	warum
wife	Ehefrau, f.
wild	wild
will, shall	werden
win	gewinnen
wind	Wind, m.
window	Fenster, n.
wine	Wein, m.
winter	Winter, m.
with	mit
without	ohne
wolf	Wolf, m.

woman	Frau, f.
work	Arbeit, f.
work	arbeiten
wren	Zaunkönig, m.
wristwatch	Armbanduhr, f.
write	schreiben
year	Jahr, n.
yellow	gelb
you (informal)	du
you (informal pl.)	ihr
you (formal)	Sie
young	jung
youngster	Jüngling, m.
your	dein
you're welcome	bitte schön
youth	Jugend, f.
zero	Null, f.

Index

Accommodations, 121–23
Accusative case, 83–86, 88
Adjectives, 52–54
    for comparisons, 113–17
    for contrasts, 108–10
    with direct objects, 84–85
    endings with, 108–17
    possessive, 103–8
Adverbial phrases, 97
Adverbs, 97
Alphabet, 2–3
Animals, 128–29
Antonyms, 108–10
Articles, 43–44, 53, 87, 107
Auxiliaries, 100–102

B, pronunciation of, 7
"Be," 55–56, 74–75
Beverages, 34
Bitten (to ask), 61–62

Cognates, 14–16
Commands, 98–100
Comparisons, 113–17
Conjunctions, 117–19
Consonants, pronunciation of, 4–7
Contrasts, 108–10
Counting, 9–13
Countries, 21–22

D, pronunciation of, 7
Das, 40–41
Dates, 22–25
Dative case, 87–90
Days, 22–23
Definite articles, 36, 40–41, 43–44, 53, 87

Der, 36, 110–13
Die, 36
Direct objects, 82–86, 90–91

Eating terms, 31–34
Ein, 62–63, 110, 112–13
Emotion words, 100–102
English language, similarities between German and, 14–16
English to German dictionary, 159–83
Essen (to eat), 58–59
Euros, 129–30

Family members, 29–31
Farewells, 19–20
Feminine nouns, 38–40, 47–48, 105–6
Food, 31–34
Formal pronouns, 51–52
Future tense, 76–77, 78, 78–79

G, pronunciation of, 7
Games, 127–28
Gender, 35–43
Genitive case, 106–8
German language, similarities between English and, 14–16
German to English dictionary, 131–57
Gestern (yesterday), 77–78
Goodbyes, 19–20
Greetings, 19–20

H, pronunciation of, 9
Haben (to have), 63–64, 75
Hand shaking, 19

Happy birthday, 24
Heute (today), 77–78
Hotels, 121–23
Hours, 26–28
Household words, 123–24
"How are you?," 20
"How" questions, 97

Idiomatic expressions, 102–3
Indefinite articles, 43–44, 87
Indirect objects, 86–91
Infinitives, 54–55
Informal pronouns, 51–52
Inseparable prefixes, 80
Interrogative words, 94–95, 119
Irregular verbs, 63–68
    future tense, 78–79
    past tense, 71–74

Kaffee und Kuchen (coffee and cake), 124–25
Kein (not any), 62–63

Language acquisition, practicing and, 1–2
Languages, 21–22
Laufen (to run), 66–67
"Like," 64–65
Long vowels, 3–4

Masculine nouns, 37–38, 43, 46–47, 105–6
Midnight, 29
Minutes, 26–28
Modal auxiliaries, 100–102
Money, 129–30
Months, 24–25
Morgen (tomorrow), 65–66, 77–78

Names, 17–18
Nationalities, 21–22
Negation, 62–63
Neuter nouns, 40–41, 48–49, 106
Nicht (not), 62
Nominative case, 83, 84–85, 88
Noon, 29
Nouns
    accusative case, 88
    dative case, 88, 88–90
    as direct objects, 82
    feminine, 38–40, 47–48, 105–6
    gender of, 35–43
    masculine, 37–38, 43, 46–47, 105–6
    neuter, 40–41, 48–49, 106
    nominative case, 88
    plural, 45–49, 106
Numbers, 9–13

Objects
    direct, 82–86, 90–91
    indirect, 86–91

Past tense, 68–76, 78
Perfect tenses, 75–76
Personal pronouns, 50–51
Phone etiquette, 20
Plural nouns, 45–49, 106
Plural pronouns, 51
Possessives, 103–8
Prefixes, 79–81
Prepositions, 85–86, 91
Present tense, 59–60, 66–68, 78
Pronouns, 49–52
    changing nouns to, 88–89
    changing nouns to, 90–91
    as direct objects, 82, 84, 86
    replacing dative nouns with, 89–90

Pronoun substitution, 50
Pronunciation
   consonants, 4–7
   letter combinations, 8–9
   practicing, 1–2
   vowels, 3–5

Questions, 93–98
   forming, 93–94
   forming, with past tense,
      70–71
   how and when, 97
   interrogative words, 94–95
   types of, 93
   where, 96–97
   who, 97–98
   why, 98

Restaurants, 31–32

Seasons, 24
Sein (to be), 55–56, 74–75
Separable prefixes, 80–81
Short vowels, 3–4
Sie, 56
Slang, 102–3
Sounds, 3–9
Spoken language, 1–2
Sports, 127–28
Sprechen (to speak), 66–67
ß (Ess-tset), 2
Subjects, 83
Superlatives, 116–17

Technology words, 125–27
Third-person pronouns, 49–50
Time, 26–29
Titles, 18
"Tomorrow," 65–66

Travel, 121–23
Trinken, 58–59

Um (at), 28
Umlaut, 3
Utensils, 34

Verbs, 54–62
   commands, 98–100
   conjugating, 54–55, 57–60,
      69–70, 74
   future tense, 76–79
   -ieren, 60–61
   irregular, 63–68, 71–74,
      78–79
   of motion, 56–58
   negation, 62–63
   past tense, 68–76, 78
   perfect tenses, 75–76
   prefixes with, 79–81
   present tense, 59–60,
      66–68, 78
   stem changes, 66–68
   tenses, 77–78
Vowels, pronunciation of, 3–5

Weekdays, 22–23
Werden (to get/to become), 68,
   75–76, 77, 78–79
"When" questions, 97
"Where" questions, 96–97
"Who" questions, 97–98
"Why" questions, 98
Wissen (to know), 66
Word order, 118–19

Years, 25
"You," 50–52